INNOCENT VICTORIAN

ARTHUR HUGH CLOUGH

by Felix W. de Weldon, sculptor
City Hall, Charleston, South Carolina
carved in Indiana limestone
1942

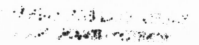

Innocent Victorian

The Satiric Poetry of Arthur Hugh Clough

Michael Timko

Ohio University Press

ℛ *Acknowledgments*

I wish to express my gratitude to various people. H. Y. Moffett and C. M. Hudson, Jr. were especially helpful during the early stages of my study ; J. H. Buckley, C. R. Woodring, and A. H. Whitley contributed time and advice during the later ones. I am also indebted to A. D. Culler and R. L. Schneider, who read parts of the manuscript and made some valuable suggestions. For the bibliography, I owe a great deal to W. E. Houghton and R. M. Gollin. I wish to acknowledge debts of various kinds to R. A. King, F. L. Mulhauser, B. B. Trawick, and J. A. Conley. For assistance in editorial matters, I should like to thank Cecil Hemley and Mark McCloskey of the Ohio University Press ; and for the indexing I should like to acknowledge publicly my debt to Mrs. John Linn. I extend my appreciation to the Dean of Graduate Studies of Queens College and his staff for the typing of the manuscript. Portions

71115

of this book have originally appeared as articles in *Victorian Poetry*, *English*, *English Studies*, and *Modern Language Quarterly*, and I wish to thank the editors of these periodicals for their gracious permission to reprint. Naturally, I have made additions and revisions, some of considerable extent, for the present text. Finally, the dedication is an attempt to indicate another debt which can never be fully repaid.

To Joy

◅ Contents

NOTES   *xiii*

Introduction   *3*

Clough's Thought   *19*

Clough's Art   *93*

Conclusion   *169*

BIBLIOGRAPHY   *177*

INDEX   *193*

He is content with the human possibility . . .

(Lionel Trilling on E. M. Forster)

It is difficult to assess Clough's work with any
finality because of the paradoxes within it. He
is in some ways a precursor of twentieth century
poetry, yet some aspects of his work make it possible
to discuss him as a poet within the eighteenth
century tradition who found himself living in the
nineteenth century. He . . . is a Janus-like poet,
both retrospective and revolutionary.

(Isobel Armstrong on Arthur Hugh Clough)

ᴥ *Notes*

Books and materials which are frequently cited are abbreviated in the following way:

PPR — Clough, Arthur Hugh, *Poems and Prose Remains,* with a Selection from His Letters and a Memoir, ed. Blanche Smith Clough. 2 vols. London, 1869.

PR — Clough, Arthur Hugh, *Prose Remains,* ed. Blanche Smith Clough. London, 1888.

Poems — *The Poems of Arthur Hugh Clough,* ed. H. F. Lowry, A. L. P. Norrington, and F. L. Mulhauser. Oxford, 1951.

Corr. — *The Correspondence of Arthur Hugh Clough,* ed. F. L. Mulhauser. 2 vols. Oxford, 1957.

Memoir — Clough, Blanche Athena, *A Memoir of Anne Jemima Clough.* London, 1897.

MSS — Manuscript materials on microfilm and in typescript at the Honnold Library in Claremont, California.

RM — *Rugby Magazine,* 2 vols. London, 1835. The best bibliographical account of *RM* and MSS is W. E. Houghton, "The

Prose Works of Arthur Hugh Clough: A Checklist and Calendar, with Some Unpublished Passages," *BNYPL,* LXIV (July, 1960), 377–394—hereafter cited as *Checklist.*

Harvard — Manuscript letters between Mrs. Clough and Charles Eliot Norton at Harvard University Library.

SPW — *Selected Prose Works of Arthur Hugh Clough,* ed. Buckner B. Trawick. University of Alabama Press, 1964.

Because my focus is mainly on Clough's thought and art, I have not stressed the biographical aspects; as a result, there may be certain events in Clough's life and works by him that should be put in some biographical context, so that the significance I attach to certain actions and writings should be evident. The following brief chronology should serve this purpose; for fuller treatments of his life Levy, Chorley and Veyriras should be consulted:

1819   —Born January 1, in Liverpool. His father, James Clough, was a cotton merchant; his mother, Anne Perfect, was the daughter of James Perfect, a banker.

1822–1828—Lived in Charleston, South Carolina.

1829–1837—At Rugby, under Dr. Arnold; various contributions to the *Rugby Magazine,* of which he was editor for a time. (See Armstrong, *Writers and Their Work, Checklist,* and *SPW* for selections from and comments on these contributions.)

1837–1848—At Oxford as student, Fellow, and Tutor; resigned in 1848.

1846   —Letters to the editor of *The Balance,* signed M.A.O.; the main interest of these lies in his ideas on social classes and political economy. (See *Checklist* and *SPW,* pp. 208–225.)

1847   —Wrote *A Consideration of Objections against the Retrenchment Association,* referred to as the Retrenchment article. (See *PPR,* I, 273–290; *SPW,* pp. 226–240.)

A good source for his "anti-aristocratic" sentiments and his agreement with Carlyle.

1848   —*The Bothie of Toper-na-Fuosich: A Long-Vacation Pastoral,* later changed to *The Bothie of Tober-na-Vuolich.*

1849   —*Ambarvalia* (with Thomas Burbidge); Clough's poems were brought out separately in 1850. Sojourn in Rome, wrote *Amours de Voyage.* Assumed duties as Principal of University Hall, London, in fall.

1850   —Met Blanche Smith; trip to Venice; wrote *Dipsychus;* also wrote at this time his review of Francis Newman's *The Soul,* which contains many of his religious ideas, and also his *Paper on Religion.* (For the dating, see *Checklist,* p. 383; for the interpolation of the *Paper on Religion* into the midst of the review, see *SPW,* p. 338; for the essays, see *PPR,* I, 293–305; *SPW,* pp. 277–288.)

1851–1852—See *Checklist* (pp. 384–388) and *SPW* (pp. 334–336) for dating and bibliographical information for lectures given at University Hall, where Clough was also Professor of English Language and Literature; of particular interest are the ones on Dryden (*PPR,* I, 329–333; *SPW,* pp. 85–106); on Wordsworth (*PPR,* I, 309–325; *SPW,* pp. 107–122); on poetry and skepticism (*SPW,* p. 123); and on the development of English literature (*PPR,* I, 337–355; *SPW,* pp. 124–142).

1852–1853—Departure from University Hall; stay in America from October, 1852, to July, 1853; did some private tutoring, wrote reviews and articles, and worked on a revision of Dryden's translation of *Plutarch's Lives* (5 vols., Boston, 1859). Other writings from this period include his review of poems by Matthew Arnold and Alexander Smith (*North American Review,* LXXVII, July, 1853, 1–30; *PPR,* I, 359–383; *SPW,* pp. 143–171), which contains his ideas on poetry; his review of his friend Charles Eliot Norton's *Considerations on Some Recent Social Theories* (*PPR*, I, 411–417; *SPW*, pp. 258–269) and his letter on might versus right in economics and politics (*SPW*, pp. 249–255), which contain many of his ideas on society; and his important *Notes on the Religious Tradition* (*PPR*, I, 421–426; *SPW*, pp. 289–293), which reveals many of his religious ideas.

1853 —Examiner in Education Office, London.

1853 —Marriage to Blanche; beginning of work for Florence Nightingale, interrupted by enforced vacations because of failing health.

1861 —Travels for health; work on *Mari Magno;* death at Florence, November 13; buried in the Protestant Cemetery.

INNOCENT VICTORIAN

❧ *Introduction*

As both man and artist Clough has not fared well at the
hands of critics; indeed, over the years the myth of the
Clough "failure" has been preserved until now the question is no longer whether Clough failed, but why he did.
Some critics have seen him as a frustrated Carlylean,
others as a frustrated satirist, others as a frustrated believer. His latest biographer, accepting the myth, finds
still another reason for his failure: Clough always had the
desire to return to the womb! Even those who have tried
to "rescue" Clough have succeeded in preserving the tradition, for they have been so intent on "defending" him,
on making him all things to all people so that he can be
acceptable, that they have managed to convey the impression that there must after all be some solid basis for the
myth. J. M. Robertson, for instance, insisted that Clough's

poetry be read as fiction, that Clough be regarded as novelist rather than poet. The latest study, Walter Houghton's *The Poetry of Clough*, keeps the focus on the poetry, but in the attempt to make Clough "contemporary" it emphasizes the "modern" techniques at the expense of the moral aesthetic that is the basis for Clough's poetry, its *raison d'être*.[1] It is as fruitless to talk of Clough's poetry from the standpoint of technique only as it is to dismiss it as fiction or to see it as the final product of a Jungian sublimation.

The undue emphasis on technique undermines Mr. Houghton's otherwise fine essay in revaluation; it enables him, for instance, to place Clough in all, often opposite, poetic camps: neoclassic, romantic, subjective, objective, modern; it leads to a serious misreading of Clough's attitude towards such important poetic characters as Claude of the *Amours de Voyage* and the hero of *Dipsychus*; it serves, finally, to preserve the myth. By failing to recognize the close connection between Clough's own life and art, between his thought and art, Mr. Houghton comes to

1. For Clough as a frustrated Carlylean see James I. Osborne, *Arthur Hugh Clough*, London, 1919; Boston, 1920, pp. 147ff., and Stanley T. Williams, "Clough's Poems," *Studies in Victorian Literature*, London, 1923, pp. 235–252; as a frustrated satirist, Humbert Wolfe, "Arthur Hugh Clough," *The Eighteen-Sixties*, London, 1932, pp. 20–50; as frustrated believer, Doris Dalglish, "Arthur Hugh Clough: The Shorter Poems," *Essays in Criticism*, II (January, 1952), 38–52; his latest biographer is Lady Katharine Chorley, *Arthur Hugh Clough: The Uncommitted Mind*, Oxford University Press, 1962; the latest study, Walter E. Houghton, *The Poetry of Clough*, New Haven and London: Yale University Press, 1963—hereafter cited as Houghton. Although Paul Veyriras's work on Clough (*Arthur Hugh Clough: 1819–1861*, Paris, 1964) is technically more recent than what I cite as the latest biography and the latest study of the poetry, I think that my meaning is clear enough. Monsieur Veyriras's work is really more of a summary of much that has been said and done in both areas—biographical and critical—and while a solid contribution in this respect, it offers nothing substantially new or strikingly different in either area.

a conclusion that is strikingly similar to that of the negative criticism against which he is ostensibly writing. To say, for instance, that "Nonetheless, like his own Dipsychus, he submitted to the Spirit," is not much different from concluding, as does Lady Chorley, "Clough became weary of the search [for truth] and abandoned it." [2]

A myth, of course, needs some basis for its inception and growth. With Clough, the materials were there, needing only certain kinds of interpretations. He was, certainly, very close to his mother during his childhood; he did attend Rugby under the great Dr. Arnold; he was at Oxford at the height of the Tractarian influence; he knew Carlyle and was influenced by many of his ideas; he read and was impressed by the higher criticism; he was unable to remain at Oxford and at University Hall, London, because of certain difficulties inherent in the positions that he held; he was unable to stay in America because of a combination of circumstances; and his last years were spent in doing what has been described as routine work. Even his poetic output is, at first sight, not overly impressive as far as quantity is concerned, and he published very little during his own lifetime. All of this, seen from special points of view, contains enough to justify some of the conclusions that have been reached.

We can, however, avoid these special points of view and see the man and his work in relation to his own time and to his own thought. Clough was either directly or indirectly involved with most of the social, political, religious, and literary movements of his time, but as yet no attempt has been made to place him and his writing—particularly his satire—in this context. "There are some

2. Houghton, p. 210; Chorley, p. 360.

writers," Hugh Walker has stated, "whose place in history is of subordinate importance. We can, if we choose, trace in their work the influence of the age in which they lived, for no man ever escaped that influence; but we are not compelled to do so. In others, the influence is absolutely vital, and unless we attend to it, we can never understand them." [3] Clough is one of these, and any study of him must necessarily include an examination of the ways in which he reacted to the "vital influences" of his age. With our clearer picture of the Victorian era, one becoming less marred by prejudice and ignorance, and with the additional information we now have of Clough's life and ideas, we are better able to see the interaction of Clough and his own age. Seen in this context, Clough emerges as a clear thinker with solid ideas and as a significant poet.

In order to understand Clough fully, we must know the quality of his thought and character. First, Clough was a Victorian, living in a period which made certain assumptions about life and art. To say this is not to say that Clough was in complete agreement with these ideas and assumptions; but the fact remains that he was influenced by and did agree with many of them, particularly so in his poetic theory and practice. Second, Clough was an artist, and to deny him this, as some have done, is to do him an injustice. He worked at his writing; he knew exactly what he was trying to do and revised and rewrote to achieve the effects that he wanted. He was also familiar with literary theory and criticism. His poetry, criticism, and writings demonstrate that he should not be dismissed as a "rough versifier" who was more interested in getting down his

3. Hugh Walker, *The Literature of the Victorian Era*, Cambridge, 1910, p. 467.

thoughts than in putting them down in the best possible way.[4] Third, it is important to recognize that in his poetic theory and practice Clough was more a Victorian than a modern, and no amount of analysis will make him a "modern." It is true that his satiric poetry reveals some "modern" tendencies, but, on the whole, Clough was committed to a poetic theory that was not too far removed from most of the accepted conventions of his day, particularly in his view of the poet and in his insistence that the poetry be "moral." Clough was not a "radical" in his poetic theory and practice.

Finally, and it is in this area that one could make a claim for "radicalism" (in the sense that he was fighting the accepted beliefs of the time), Clough had ideas, and very positive ones, on the major concerns of his age, ideas that form the foundation for much of his satiric poetry and many of his actions during his lifetime. Living in an age when conformity, custom, and convention seemed to play a dominant part in man's life, Clough insisted on the importance of "the natural" over the artificial, on the real over the false. It is true, of course, that other Victorian writers were doing this, but what distinguishes Clough most clearly from his contemporaries is the basis of his thought, his "positive naturalism." What makes him significant in our day, and also marks his unique contribution

4. For a summary of Cloughian criticism up to the present time see Walter Houghton, "Arthur Hugh Clough: A Hundred Years of Disparagement," *Studies in English Literature,* I (Autumn, 1961), 30–61. One school, for instance, claims that Clough was concerned more with the thoughts than with the form of his poems, and that he simply could not bring these ideas under artistic control; another says that Clough was not concerned with form. For the first see Charles Whibley, "Introduction" to *Poems,* London, 1913, pp. ix–xxxvii; for the second see Lionel Johnson, *Academy,* XXXIX (January 10, 1891), 31–32.

to his own, is his "acceptance of the human fact as we know it now." Like E. M. Forster, another writer who has also failed to gain wide acceptance, Clough is "that remarkably rare being, a naturalist whose naturalism is positive and passionate, not negative, passive and apologetic for man's nature." [5] It is this quality, revealed most fully in his satiric poetry, that sets him apart from his contemporaries and gives to his writing its distinctiveness, its sense of immediacy, and its feeling of rightness.

"It is the virtue of man to know and love the ideal. / It is the wisdom of man to accept and love the real," Clough once wrote, and it is this love and acceptance that make his writing seem so fresh and vital today. In an age of "compromise" Clough refused to advocate easy solutions or timid compromises. In this respect, certainly, he is a realist whose positive qualities have not yet been fully recognized. Dissatisfied with life about him, as were most of his contemporaries, Clough, unlike some others, still retained his "innocence" and a firm belief in the "native goodness" of human nature and the dignity of the human spirit.

It is at this point that misunderstandings of Clough's thought and art often arise. His acceptance of human nature, his refusal to deal in absolutes, to condemn on rigid moral and ethical grounds, are taken to be signs of weakness or lack of conviction. This has often led to misinterpretations of his poems, particularly "It fortifies my soul to know," "*Epi-Strauss-ium,*" the two parts of the "Easter Day" poem, and *Dipsychus,* the "submission" of

5. Lionel Trilling, *E. M. Forster,* New Directions Books, Norfolk, Conn., 1943, pp. 22, 23. My debt to the first chapter in this book, "Forster and the Liberal Imagination," is great.

whose hero has consistently been misjudged. Clough's refusal to be arbitrary also has been seen as a sign of a total
objectivity, an indication of his willingness only to point
out difficulties rather than to suggest positive solutions as
well. Again, although Clough was able to see both (or all)
sides of a question, he was writing with a firm moral commitment, not with the intent merely to display verbal wit
or poetic pyrotechnics. At the core of his life and work are
a resiliency and toughness and an integrity found in few
others writing during his own time.

Certainly it would have been easier to allow himself to
be seduced by alien visions or by such high-sounding
words as "custom," "authority," or "tradition." It would
have been much simpler to resort to "base mechanical
adroitness." However, Clough recognized and tried to
demonstrate in his writing that man also had within him
this "interfering, enslaving, o'ermastering demon of craving," as well as nobility, honor, and the capacity for love
and endurance. It is precisely this recognition that makes
the term "positive naturalism" so fitting; for, in addition
to his insistence on man's need to pursue the "truth" and
his belief in the "essence" of Christianity, Clough was also
a "naturalist" who refused to deny the validity of man's
emotions and desires, "natural" as well as ideal. He was
also positive in this naturalism with his insistence that
these emotions and desires, when given full recognition and
not suppressed, could lead to a fuller and more satisfying
life here on earth. It is because of this view that he insists
that we stop dreaming of what might be and work with
what we have. Man's salvation depends not on illusion, but
on reality, not on creating new heavens for himself, but on
making the best of this world. The quality that makes

Clough a significant Victorian is his clear recognition of the paradoxical, yet ultimately admirable, nature of man.

The essential concern of the Victorian period might be described in the same terms that Robert Corrigan describes the task of modern playwrights: "looking for a metaphor that is symbolic of the inalienable part of every man—that irreducible part of each of us which exists after all the differences have been stripped away, and which is beyond and beneath all that is social, political, economic, religious, and ideological." [6] Now to many Victorians this approach would be unintelligible, for they tended to see man as religious, or social, or economic, or political, not simply as human. It was against this restrictive view that Arnold, for instance, was writing his essays on sweetness and light and the dissidence of dissent. Even Arnold, however, tended at times to think of and write about man as a creature wandering between two worlds. Clough also saw man in these various contexts, but his most consistent view of man was not as a displaced person but as one who simply had not yet come to the recognition of his own nature, his "inmost I."

To Clough, man, as a human, necessarily has to suffer, but he also has to grow. "Earthy as well as godlike," he is bound to develop until his native goodness asserts itself and he learns to live as befits him. Clough was keenly aware of that "irreducible part of each of us." In his *Mystery of the Fall*, an artistic failure but a valuable poem for providing insight into his thought, Clough has Adam try to describe this very idea:

6. *The New Theatre of Europe*, ed. with an intro. by Robert W. Corrigan, Delta Books, 1962, p. 9.

>   *yet still*
> *I, or a something that is I indeed,*
> *A living, central, and more inmost I*
> *Within the scales of mere exterior me's,*
> *I—seem eternal, O thou God, as Thou;*
>   (*Poems*, p. 415)

And Clough's "metaphor that is symbolic of the inalienable part of every man" is one that indicates clearly his optimistic attitude towards human nature, for his imagery concerning man is usually that of growing, natural objects, such as seeds, trees, and flowers. Adam tells Eve:

> *That which we were, we could no more remain*
> *Than in the moist provocative vernal mould*
> *A seed its suckers close, and rest a seed.*
> *We were to grow.*
>   (*Poems*, p. 410)

In this characteristic image Clough indicates both his realistic appraisal of the world, with its "vernal provocativeness," and his optimistic faith in man's eventual development and full maturity as a human being. And his concern is always with man in this world, the here and now; the focus is always on "the contradictions, paradoxes and dangers of living the moral life," and the intention is "the better understanding of the inextricable tangle of good and evil and of how perilous moral action can be." Like Forster, again, Clough was "cursed with the Primal Curse, which is not the knowledge of good and evil, but the knowledge of good-and-evil." [7] With this view, Clough was able to transcend the Victorian morality, and is therefore

7. *Forster*, pp. 11–12.

able to speak to us today in a manner that is both convincing and attractive.

Clough's positive naturalism explains one puzzle that many critics have been unable to solve: the high esteem in which he was held by others. "Those who knew him well," wrote Stanley in the *Daily News* of January 9, 1862, "knew that in him a genius and character of no common order has passed away, but they will scarcely be able to justify their knowledge to a doubting world." That these were not merely words spoken in a spirit of condolence is illustrated by the testimony of others, including such diverse figures as Charles Eliot Norton, James Russell Lowell, Francis Newman, Tom Arnold, R. H. Hutton, Walter Bagehot, Ralph Waldo Emerson, Matthew Arnold, and Thomas Carlyle. Frederick Temple looked upon Clough as "the ablest and greatest man" he had ever come across, and the one from whom he had learned more than any other man he had known. Benjamin Jowett, not one to praise lightly, regarded Clough as a person gifted with a great deal of genius. Archibald Campbell Tait saw Clough in the same light. Furious at Clough's getting a second class degree, he remarked: "They had not only a first rate scholar, but a man of original genius before them, and were too stupid to discover it." Carlyle perhaps best expressed the general feeling when he described Clough as "a diamond sifted out of the general rubbish-heap." [8]

Stanley's fear that those who knew Clough well would have difficulty in conveying his particular genius to a

8. E. G. Sandford, ed., *Memoirs of Archbishop Temple by Seven Friends,* 2 vols., London and New York, 1906, I, 52; R. T. Davidson and William Benham, eds., *Life of Archbishop Tait,* 2 vols., London, 1884, I, 457–458. For a good summary of the esteem in which Clough was held see Chorley, pp. 2–4.

doubting world seems justified, for Clough's personality and distinctive point of view still remain an enigma; yet, there is other evidence to support his positive qualities: the evidence of his thought and art. His positive naturalism is nowhere more apparent than in the responses he makes to the problems of his age, particularly those brought on by the changes taking place in the social, political, economic, and religious spheres. Change has been cited as the dominant characteristic of the Victorian period; [9] and it is Clough's ability to retain his realistic view of human nature in the face of this change and to assert consistently and positively his principles that characterizes his work and makes his contribution to Victorian literature so significant. Sensitive, sympathetic, perceptive, at times brilliantly witty, at others bitterly ironic, Clough was able to see through the thick smoke that covered the battleground of Victorian controversy and to distinguish the real—i.e., the true. The consistent theme of his work is his condemnation of the false, the artificial, the insincere, and his praise for the real, the natural, the good.

This approach is pervasive in all of his writing. In the political sphere, both domestic and international, he refused to be trapped into accepting either of the attractive extremes of complete freedom or authoritarianism; he was, instead, a "liberal of the future," [10] concerned not with systems or parties but with the individual's relationship to others and with the development of the human spirit. Avoiding jingoism or paternalism, Clough insisted that a government was to be judged only on the basis of its

9. Walter Houghton, *The Victorian Frame of Mind,* New Haven and London, Yale University Press, 1957, p. 1.

10. Francis W. Palmer, "Was Clough a Failure?" *Philological Quarterly,* XXII (January, 1943), 63.

granting "genuine liberty" to its people. Hence his condemnation of both parties in England, each of which
seemed to be interested only in furthering its own fortunes; his support of the Italians against the Austrians;
and his disgust with Napoleon III, who seemed to him the
symbol of tyranny and oppression. His statements on
social and economic questions were predicated on the same
principles that inspired his political ideas: a sincere sympathy for those suffering from oppression and a genuine
desire to serve and help them. Disturbed by the pernicious
philosophy underlying laissez-faire, the thought of placing relationships of individuals on a cash-nexus basis only,
Clough insisted on the need for new definitions of liberty.
Basing his solutions on the essential dignity of the human
spirit, Clough refused to view men as "hands" or "ma-
chines" or "servants"; from the vantage point of his hu-
mane realism, he insisted that men combine for higher
objects than the mere "culinary" one of securing equal
apportionments of meat and drink. Service, not liberty,
equality, or fraternity, was the watchword.

Clough's avoidance of unreasonable dogmatism and
irrational emotion, his insistence on knowledge and reasonableness are seen to best advantage in his comments on religion, perhaps the area that caused the most violent reactions in the Victorian period. It is also in this area that
Clough's distinction between natural and artificial is most
evident. For Clough, the great gap between religion and
life was the heart of the matter. Religious experiences of
all types seemed to prove that religion was sadly impracticable in daily life, and the problem became one of the
necessary adjustment (not compromise) between the two.

In his attempts to show the results of religious hypocrisy that enabled people to place great emphasis on outward forms and customs and make no attempt to come to a genuine understanding of the true meaning and spirit behind them, Clough consistently stressed the necessity to make religion not a theological creed, but a way of life. Basic to this point of view was, again, his recognition that man did not need to look for new virtues, but needed to order and distribute his native goodness in this world. One of the statements that Clough has the hero of the poem *Dipsychus* make is especially significant in the context of his own belief: "It seems His newer will/ We should not think of Him at all, but trudge it,/ And of the world He has assigned us make/ What best we can." To Clough this was more than just a poetic utterance; it summed up his religious position.

It is against this intellectual and philosophic background that his satiric poetry needs to be examined, for the lack of emphasis given to Clough's positive naturalism has had an unfortunate effect on his reputation as an artist. What is meaningful and vital in Clough's poetry is not the employment of some techniques that have become prominent in modern poetry, but the philosophic attitude that forms the basis of his poetry, an attitude that reveals his view of the role of the poet and the place of poetry in life itself. Living in an age that demanded "moral" poetry, Clough responded, but with moral realism rather than didactic moralizing. Writing in an age that demanded "communication," Clough responded by creating a poetic based on what he regarded as the best from the past and present, a poetic that determined the subject matter, diction, imagery, and, most significantly perhaps, the genres in which he wrote: the lyric and satire.[11]

Some attempts have been made to see these two strains in Clough's poetry as being opposed to one another; but, while some valid distinction may be made concerning his practice in the two forms, they are both the products of his own poetic. Both reveal his belief that poetry should deal with the here and now. Both demonstrate his concern that poetry be a criticism of life, that it interpret the significance of our actions in universal rather than particular terms. Finally, both illustrate his handling of imagery, diction, and style, all of which reflect the essentially moral bias of his poetry.

What needs to be stressed, however, is that in actual practice Clough came closest to his ideal in his satire, the genre that illustrates even more clearly than the lyric the moral realism and stylistic characteristics so distinctly his.[12] The lyrics, in which he was intent on depicting the universality of the inner conflicts of human beings, are written for the most part in traditional forms and reflect the qualities of his character: simplicity, self-control, sincerity. The satires, however, in which he was concerned more with the exploration of the individual's relationship with the religious, social, and aesthetic environment of his time and with the demonstration of his deep concern over man's failure to measure up to the standards of his positive naturalism, are more distinctly Cloughian. Modifying,

11. On this point of the need to create a poetic, see Stephen Spender, "The Voice of Honest Doubt," *The Sunday Times* (London), 3 Nov., 1957, p. 10; and Valerie Pitt, *Tennyson Laureate,* London, 1962, pp. 252ff.

12. Significant in this respect is Buckner B. Trawick's insistence on Clough's pre-eminence as a "thinker." "Without minimizing his lyrical ability," he writes, "one may fairly say that it is as a logician and an alert observer of facts that Clough excelled." (*SPW*, p. 15)

but not completely rejecting, the Tennysonian style of his age, with its musical regularity and poetic diction, he wrote his satiric poems in a vigorous, masculine style, employing irony, ambiguity, and indirection, techniques particularly suited to the dialectic of the genre. While his lyrics deserve more attention than they have up to now received, especially for the light that they shed on his poetic theory, his satiric poems deserve even more, for they reveal quite clearly the artistic and intellectual depth of his aesthetic and moral vision.

Whether Clough deserves to be more highly regarded as artist and thinker than he has been up to now is a valid area for exploration. The biographical and critical studies that have been devoted to him have been limited to the extent that they have failed to stress his satiric poems and have failed to examine his work in the context of his own day and his own thought. To stress and examine that genre which reflects both his mature thought and art would seem to be a right step in the direction of fruitful investigation.

✒ Clough's Thought

(A) The religious position

The Victorian period, one of the most complex in English history, was especially characterized by a profound spiritual unrest, brought about mainly by the far-reaching discoveries of science and Biblical criticism. One recent essay has emphasized the "disintegration of Christian thought" as one of the significant ways in which this period is different from any previous period in modern history, while another has singled out "the disappearance of God" as one of the most important themes in Victorian poetry.[1] It is no wonder, then, that the age gave rise to

---

1. Walter Houghton, "The Victorian Period" in *British Literature from Blake to the Present Day,* ed. Hazelton Spencer, Walter E. Houghton, Herbert Barrows, 2nd ed., Boston, 1963, p. 368; J. Hillis

varieties of religious experience covering the spectrum
from atheism to mysticism, from extreme rationalism to
devout idealism. It was an age of perplexed prophets in
which each man was forced to re-examine the foundations
of his beliefs before making his declaration of faith.

In broad terms, the conflict can be seen as one between
empiricism and idealism, naturalism and supernaturalism
(for want of a better term), or science and faith. More
specifically, the enemies of orthodox faith could be recognized (with different degrees of hostility or horror) in
such varied movements and beliefs as Utilitarianism,
Deism, Pantheism, Unitarianism, and the Religion of
Humanity; in the attacks on the Bible by "higher critics,"
who were subjecting the Book to tests of scientific, literary, and historical criticism, just as scholars had always
examined other famous works; and in the terrifying discoveries of science, the results of which were undermining
the belief in the infallibility of the Scriptures. Within the
Church of England the problems were also serious and
disturbing. Besides the traditional differences with the
Roman Catholics on the right and the Dissenters on the
left, there was friction within the Church itself. The Evangelical or Low Church, with its Methodist "enthusiasm,"
was on the left; the Tractarians or Puseyites, with their
Roman leanings, were on the right; and the Liberal or
Broad Church, which too often seemed to be nodding in the
direction of the higher critics and the scientists, was somewhere in the middle. It is against this background that
Matthew Arnold was able to say, "There is not a creed

Miller, "The Theme of the Disappearance of God in Victorian Poetry,"
Victorian Studies, VI (March, 1963), 207–227. See his *The Disappearance of God: Five Nineteenth-Century Writers,* Cambridge, Mass., 1963.

which is not shaken; not an accredited dogma which is not shown to be questionable." [2]

The question of where Clough fits into this spectrum is an important one, for it has a direct bearing on the interpretation of his poetry and the actions he took at various times during his own lifetime. As might be expected, during this period emotion sometimes overruled objective judgment, and general terms like skeptic and doubter were applied to many, sometimes with little attempt to qualify or define. "During the decade after his [Clough's] death," Palmer noted, "in the excitement that followed publication of Darwin's theory of natural selection, everyone was ranged without qualification in the ranks of Faith or ranks of Doubt." [3] Clough came to be classed as a doubter and skeptic, and the classification still persists.

Illustrations of this approach are not hard to find. F. L. Lucas stated that Clough "remains the impersonation of an age when religious doubt was not, as now, a rare and mild greensickness, but a crippling, even a fatal malady." H. V. Routh wrote that Clough "persistently searched for some definite idea or cause in which his whole being could find its scope, but without success." Discussing Clough's prose, Stanley T. Williams concluded that Clough was "first and always, the doubter. . . . Clough remained until his death a perplexed spirit." More recently, Kingsbury Badger has remarked on Clough's "submission," his finding it easier to drift than to throw himself into active living and writing, because of his allowing "reason to become . . . tyrannical over the other elements of human

2. Matthew Arnold, *Essays in Criticism:* Second Series, London, 1888; London, 1894, p. 1.
3. Palmer, "Was Clough a Failure?" pp. 58–59.

nature." [4] Even when Clough is not outrightly classified in this way, he is placed in some vague category of "Theist" or "believer" or "Transcendentalist," with the implication that, as earnestly as he tried, he was unable to overcome the doubts and conflicts of his time. No matter what the approach, it seems, Clough emerges as "an important and rather touching and rather annoying exhibit at the inquest on early Victorian faith or scepticism or whatever it was." [5]

Most notable in all these judgments of Clough's religious position is the lack of recognition of his moral realism, a certain unwillingness or inability to give full weight to his distinctive outlook. The point made by Badger about Clough's artistic achievement, that it was "at once the product of the peculiar Victorian environment and of his own peculiar temperament," might also be made of his religious position. [6] His peculiar Victorian environment is reflected in the successive influences under which he came through his mother, Dr. Thomas Arnold, J. H. Newman, Thomas Carlyle, and the higher criticism. His peculiar temperament is seen in the manner in which he reacted to these various influences, never being completely dominated by any one, but always taking from each only that which he considered to be lasting and helpful. The result was a religious position that both reflects and transcends the Victorian age. Rather than evidences of "submission," Clough's actions and writing are proofs of one who at last

4. F. L. Lucas, "Clough," *Eight Victorian Poets,* Cambridge, 1930; *Ten Victorian Poets,* Cambridge, 1940, p. 73; H. V. Routh, *Towards the Twentieth Century,* New York, 1937, p. 170; Williams, p. 238; Kingsbury Badger, "Arthur Hugh Clough as Dipsychus," *Modern Language Quarterly,* XXI (March, 1951), 54.

5. T. E. Welby, "Clough," *Back Numbers,* New York, 1929, p. 109.

6. Badger, p. 52.

"beat his music out" and found "a stronger faith his own." From all that he did and wrote, we find emerging a definite religious pattern, centered around positive ideas on God, Christianity, and duty, and firmly based on his acceptance of human nature for what it is, rather than what it might have been or will become.

Before he came under the influence of Carlyle, Clough's conception of God had been largely derived from his mother and Dr. Arnold. From his mother, who read the Bible regularly to her children and made sure that they attended church regularly, Clough received the picture of God as a Heavenly Father, one who was always looking out for his children. Later on, when he went to Rugby, Clough came under the direct influence of Dr. Arnold, who, in spite of Newman's doubt, was a devout and sincere Christian with a powerful and deep faith in a personal God. From Arnold, Clough received encouragement in two directions that his mother would have found distasteful. On the one hand, Dr. Arnold, with his own rejection of a completely anthropomorphic notion of God as a "magnified and non-natural man," gave to Clough the first hint that God as a father-image was not a completely satisfying concept.[7] On the other, with his typically paradoxical attitude towards questions of religion, Arnold gave to his pupil the idea of God as stern Judge. The seriousness with which he took Arnold's teaching to heart may be seen from the letters he wrote to his brother George from Rugby. "You must not," he told him in one, "think of God [as] only your loving Father and Friend . . . but

7. E. L. Williamson, Jr., "Matthew Arnold's 'Eternal Not Ourselves . . . ,' " *Modern Language Notes,* LXXV (April, 1960), 309–312. See also his *The Liberalism of Thomas Arnold,* University of Alabama Press, 1964.

also as your Judge, as one who is so holy and pure that he cannot bear any sin in this world of his, and who at the same time is so powerful as to be able to inflict the heaviest punishments." (*Corr.*, I, 27; *PPR*, I, 63)

But when Clough moved on to Oxford in 1837, at the height of the Tractarian movement, he was subjected to new and conflicting influences, and all his religious beliefs underwent sharp revision. Much has been made of Dr. Arnold's adverse influence on Clough, but the fact is that it was the "intellectual deliverance" that Clough received at Rugby that enabled Clough to meet and solve positively the problems he later faced at Oxford. Arnold's teaching helped him overcome his earlier narrow views, for perhaps the greatest gift he had received from Arnold was the desire to think for himself and follow his thoughts to their logical conclusions. In all his teaching, Arnold's one aim was to give his students the faculty of independent judgment on all questions. "His whole method was founded on the principle of awakening the intellect of every individual boy," Stanley wrote. "He not only laid great stress on original compositions, but endeavored so to choose the subjects of exercises as to oblige them to read and lead them to think for themselves." If one keeps Clough in mind, perhaps the most revealing statement by Stanley is the following: "It was always his wish that his pupils should form their own opinions for themselves, and not take them on trust from him. . . . Though no particular school of opinion grew up amongst them, the end of his teaching would be answered far more truly . . . if his scholars learned to form an independent judgment for themselves, and to carry out their opinions to their legitimate conse-

quences." [8] Thus when Clough came in contact with the
Tractarian influence and with the ideas of the German
higher critics, especially those of Strauss, and of men like
Arnold himself and Carlyle, he was able not only to form
independent judgments about them, but he proceeded to
carry them out to their legitimate consequences even more
thoroughly and more fearlessly than Arnold himself.
What has been interpreted as a period of aimless wandering in Clough's life was really the period during which he
was absorbing new influences and qualifying old beliefs.
He was perplexed for a time, it is true, but when he resigned from Oxford in 1848, he already had gained the
basic religious ideas that were to serve him the rest of his
life.

His view of God was one of these. Of the voices that
came to him out of the "vortex of philosophism and discussion" at Oxford, one of the most prominent was that of
Thomas Carlyle. Clough did not meet Carlyle until later,
but while at Oxford he had begun reading Carlyle's works,
and their great influence may be seen in Clough's letters,
poems, and essays of these and later years. The change in
his concept of the nature of God is particularly evident in
the poetry written at Oxford. Once he had been given the
slightest clue concerning the dangers of applying the
ideas of personality to God, a clue supplied by Arnold, it
was a logical step to believe with Carlyle that man can
know absolutely nothing of the nature of God and that
any attempt to define Him is either foolish or hypocritical.
Carlyle, attempting to combat the "mechanistic" con-

8. Arthur P. Stanley, *The Life and Correspondence of Thomas Arnold,* London, 1844; London, 1858, pp. 126, 127–128.

cept of the universe, had written: "The ALMIGHTY MAKER is not like a Clockmaker," and "the faith in an Invisible, Unnameable, Godlike, present everywhere in all we see and work and suffer, is the essence of all faith whatsoever." Clough echoes these words, first condemning the mechanistic idea of the universe in "When Israel Came Out of Egypt":

> And as of old from Sinai's top
>   God said that God is One,
> By Science strict so speaks He now
>   To tell us, There is None!
>
> Earth goes by chemic forces; Heaven's
>   A Mécanique Céleste!
> And heart and mind of human kind
>   A watch-work as the rest!
>
> (*Poems*, p. 17)

and then in "*Qui Laborat, Orat*," demonstrating his anti-anthropomorphism:

> With eye down-dropt, if then this earthly mind
>   Speechless remain, or speechless e'en depart;
> Nor seek to see—for what of earthly kind
>   Can see Thee as Thou art?—
>
> (*Poems*, p. 13)

"O not unowned, Thou shalt unnamed forgive," he concludes. God exists; that is all man is able to say. "God, unidentified, was thought-of still," he wrote in an early Oxford poem, "Blank Misgivings," I; the line is significant as an indication of his belief in God, which he never lost, and the inability of man to perceive the nature of this God.[9]

Once he had come to regard God in this light, Clough never changed this view, and it is demonstrated time and again in his later writings. In his *Paper on Religion* he rejected flatly the concept of God as a kind of master technician or chief engineer. "You have found out God, have you?" he asks. "The vessel goes on its way. . . . You conclude there is some one somewhere working those wheels, those pistons. . . ." He then brings his ironic wit into play: "Oh my friends, and if in a dark room under the main deck you have hunted out a smudgy Personage with a sub-intelligent look about the eyes,—is that so great a gospel for me? . . . Am I therefore to fall down and worship?" (*SPW*, p. 287; *PPR*, I, 301–302) His refusal to entertain any notion of a God created in man's image is also evident, for he attributes this idea to an overwrought imagination or to superstition. "Is it safe," he asks, "to ascribe an objective actual character to any picture of our imagination even in highest moments of beatitude?" (*SPW*, p. 282; *PPR*, I, 299)

Yet it would be a mistake to conclude, as have various critics, that Clough's God is merely "an impersonal force, operant either in the laws of nature or in the moral law," or that his final position was some kind of hazy Theism.[10]

9. Thomas Carlyle, *Past and Present, Works,* Boston, n.d., XIX, 144. For Clough and Carlyle see *Corr.,* I, 93, 96, 106, 153, 274; II, 365, 409, 529; Maurice Hewlett, "Teufelsdröckh in Hexameters," *Nineteenth Century and After,* XCI (January, 1922), 68–75, reprinted in *Extemporary Essays,* London, 1922, pp. 176–187; Kathleen Tillotson, *Matthew Arnold and Carlyle,* London, 1956; item 47 in *Checklist,* p. 389; and *SPW,* pp. 249–255.

10. Palmer, "The Bearing of Science on the Thought of Arthur Hugh Clough," *PMLA,* LIX (March, 1944), 223; see also Townsend Scudder, "Incredible Recoil," *American Scholar* (Winter, 1936), pp. 35–48.

Certainly he avoids Matthew Arnold's rather impersonal depiction of "an eternal power not ourselves that makes for righteousness," as well as Carlyle's vague Godlike presence. Although Clough depicts the Deity as unfathomable, there are present in his references to God a sincerity of tone and a warmth of feeling that dispel any cold objectivity or impersonality. Lyrics like *"Qui Laborat, Orat,"* "When Israel Came Out of Egypt," "What we, when face to face we see," and especially "O thou whose image in the shrine" reflect this sincerity and warmth:

> *O thou, in that mysterious shrine*
> *Enthroned, as we must say, divine!*
> *I will not frame one thought of what*
> *Thou mayest either be or not.*
> *I will not prate of 'thus' and 'so,'*
> *And be profane with 'yes' and 'no.'*
> *Enough that in our soul and heart*
> *Thou, whatso'er thou may'st be, art.*
>
> (*Poems*, p. 88)

As Palmer notes, Clough never abandoned the use of the word God; thus, it would seem that somewhere between the two extremes of a personal God created in man's image (one thinks of Browning immediately) and an impersonal force lies Clough's concept of God. Characteristically, he refused to bow completely either to reason or emotion. The closest he ever came to giving a precise definition to the Deity was in his use of the term *truth* as a synonym for God. In a poem written early in his Oxford career he spoke of "the vital atmosphere of Truth/ Where He again is visible" (*Poems*, p. 26), and in another written about the same time he asked for the "higher courage" that enabled

one to show the "truly right." (*Poems*, p. 10) The word
truth did not have for Clough the stoical quality that some
critics have attempted to give it; to him its connotations
were much more emotional and "religious." It is precisely
for this reason that the lyric "It fortifies my soul to know"
(*Poems*, p. 75) is much more central to Clough's religious
belief than has been recognized up to now. Rather than a
"stoical understatement," it in fact sums up his faith in
God:

> *It fortifies my soul to know*
> *That, though I perish, Truth is so:*
> *That, howsoe'er I stray and range,*
> *Whate'er I do, Thou dost not change.*
> *I steadier step when I recall*
> *That, if I slip, Thou dost not fall.*
> (*Poems*, p. 75)

It is with this idea of "truth" in mind that his use of the
word must be judged, no matter what the immediate context. When Claude of the *Amours de Voyage* speaks of the
truth as being "the Truth as ever," and when Clough in
"Easter Day," II speaks of the "true" creed, the statements involve more than an intellectual or even ethical concern; and while all this may seem much too vague to some,
from Clough's point of view it would be a perversion of
man's reason and a capitulation to superstition to be more
definite about the Deity.

There is nothing vague, however, about Clough's belief
in the "essence" of Christianity, for his firm faith in these
essential truths was the result of his doing away with what
he considered to be the main obstacles to a wholehearted
support of the Christian religion, obstacles that were due

to either "vague mysticism" or a foolish insistence that one
must believe all the historical facts of Christianity or not
be a Christian. Avoiding either blind worship or author-
itarian dogmatism, Clough was able to arrive at a position
from which he was able to believe that although historical
and scientific criticism had made uncertain its historical
accuracy, there was still enough essential truth in Christianity to make it the "best of all religions." For him, as
for Carlyle, the "soul" of Christianity was eternally true;
it was only the mortal body with which it had been pro-
vided that was perishing.

Up to the time he went to Oxford there is no reason to
believe that Clough was anything but an orthodox Angli-
can, although Dr. Arnold had planted some seeds that
were to bear strange fruit later on. When Clough entered
Balliol in 1837, the Oxford Movement was at its height,
and Clough was for a time subjected, but never seriously
in danger of succumbing, to its subtle appeal. John Henry
Newman, its accepted leader, was Vicar of St. Mary's and
preaching his impressive and moving sermons against "the
slackness of fibre in the religious life; against the poverty,
softness, restlessness, worldliness, the blunted and im-
paired sense of professing Christianity; . . . the strange
blindness to the real sternness, nay the austerity of the
New Testament." [11] The *Tracts for the Times* were also
being circulated, and their various topics were being discussed, argued, and debated, so that Clough was immediately plunged into this religious speculation and excitement. "If it had not been for the Class List, which kept a
certain number of us working at classics and mathe-

---

11. R. W. Church, *The Oxford Movement,* London, 1891; London,
1932, pp. 21–22.

matics," wrote one of his contemporaries, "the University would have become a mere battlefield of theologians." [12]

Clough had come to Oxford ready to help reform the place which contained the "Oxford Malignants," as the title of Dr. Arnold's essay had termed them, but he soon found himself attracted to Newman, who, like Dr. Arnold, had a magnetic personality. Who could resist, wrote Matthew Arnold, "the charm of that spiritual apparition, gliding in the dim afternoon light through the aisles of St. Mary's, rising into the pulpit, and then, in the most entrancing of voices, breaking the silence with words and thoughts which were a religious music,—subtle, sweet, mournful?" Newman's magnetism reached Clough. "Have you ever read Newman's Sermons?" he asked his friend Simpkinson. "I hope you will soon if you have not, for they are very good and I should [think] especially useful for us." (*Corr.*, I, 66) To Gell he wrote in April that he wished the former were at Oxford, where he would have "a good chance of becoming a disciple of [the great Newman] whom I like much better than I did and admire in many points exceedingly." (*Corr.*, I, 69; *PPR*, I, 79) Besides hearing Newman's sermons, Clough also met him personally at other times, once at a dinner party, and again at a small, select breakfast, where, he told Gell, "I was introduced, and had the honour of drinking wine with him: on the strength of all which of course, as is one's bounden duty, I must turn Newmanist." (*Corr.*, I, 88; *PPR*, I, 79)

Besides Newman himself, the greatest Tractarian influence on Clough at Oxford was his direct, personal contact with W. G. Ward, his mathematics tutor. Ward, too, had

12. H. F. Lowry, *The Letters of Matthew Arnold to Arthur Hugh Clough*, New York, 1932, p. 16.

been a pupil of Arnold's at Rugby, but at Oxford he had
become one of the leaders of the Newmanists. Delighting
in argument and philosophic discussion, Ward began to
engage Clough in discussion at every opportunity. "If
you were to come here," Clough told Gell, "you would at
once have Ward at you asking you your opinions on every
possible subject." (*Corr.*, I, 85; *PPR*, I, 79) Although
Ward was a very good friend, Clough soon had to impose
strict limitations upon their relationship, for, as he told
Simpkinson in October, 1839, he hoped to escape "the vortex of Philosophism and Discussion, (whereof Ward is the
Centre), as it is the most exhausting exercise in the
world." (*Corr.*, I, 97; *PPR*, I, 84)

Nevertheless, the attraction of Newman's personality
and the close contact with Ward naturally drew Clough
into an examination of the various beliefs and dogmas of
the Tractarians. In 1838, on Monday of Passion Week, he
recorded in his diary: "I must keep in mind . . . that
many persons of the most advanced piety and goodness are
this week engaged in all sorts of self-denial, and mortifica-
tion . . . —Newman for instance, whose errors as we believe them to be must not make me ever forget how far he is
above me in goodness and piety, and wisdom too." (Lowry,
p. 14) A short time later he contrasted the Tractarian
ideas to those of the Evangelicals:

> And it is no harm but rather good to give oneself up a
> little to hearing Oxford people, and admiring their good
> points, which lie, I suppose, principally in all they hold
> in opposition to the Evangelical portion of society—the
> benefit and beauty and necessity of forms—the ugliness
> of feelings put on unnaturally soon and consequently
> kept up by artificial means, ever strained and never

sober. I should think very likely too their Anti-Calvin-
istic Views of Justification were very, if not just, at least
useful to lead us to the Truth.

(*Corr.*, I, 71; *PPR*, I, 76–77)

But there were some points that Clough could not bring
himself to admire: "I should be very sorry ever to be
brought to believe their further views of matter acting on
morals as a charm of sacramentalism, and the succession-
notion so closely connected with it. All this, and their way
of reading and considering Scripture—such a contrast to
the German fashions—rests I suppose entirely on their
belief in the Infallibility of the Church down to a certain
period." (*Corr.*, I, 71; *PPR*, I, 77)

The "German fashion" of reading and considering
Scripture is the clue to Clough's real development at Oxford, for the German criticism was a much more vital influence on him than the Tractarian one. His contact with
German philosophical, scientific, and historical criticism,
particularly his readings in Goethe, Schiller, and Kant,
made a deep impression; and these, but even more particularly the various findings of the Tübingen School, con-
vinced him that he needed to re-examine his basic beliefs.
"He became acquainted with the writings of the Tübingen
School," Thomas Arnold wrote, "and seems to have held
that the mythical theory of Strauss, and the New Testament of Baur, were alike unanswerable." [13] Like Dr. Arnold, Clough was also affected by Niebuhr's *History of
Rome*, but, unlike Arnold, he felt that there was nothing
wrong with submitting the evidence of religion to the same

13. Thomas Arnold, "Arthur Hugh Clough: A Sketch," *The Nineteenth Century and After*, XLIII (January, 1898), 115; Mrs. Humphry
Ward, *A Writer's Recollections*, 2 vols., London, 1918, esp. I, 15–18.

tests that Niebuhr had applied to secular subjects. Arnold
wanted to restrict inquiry to questions of science, history,
and criticism; Clough was not able to make any distinction
between the intellectual and spiritual. If the German critics
pointed out facts that contradicted the orthodox views,
Clough would not ignore these facts. And, if these facts
were indeed true and made it necessary, he was ready to
review many of his orthodox views, and indeed did.

Clough's belief in the "essence" of Christianity reflects
his positive attitude towards the higher criticism. As early
as 1835, while still at Rugby, he had been guided by the
words and example of Dr. Arnold to begin thinking that
true help for the Christian religion lay in the lessening of
differences among sects and the strengthening of their
beliefs in the essentials of the religion.[14] At Oxford, this
belief grew stronger as he found support for it in the
higher criticism, which he came to regard, unlike so many
Victorians, not as a means of attack upon Christianity,
but as a means to a truer knowledge of it. He condemned
any criticism that sought merely to destroy rather than to
aid faith, citing, for instance, that criticism which simply
pointed out inconsistencies in Biblical accounts. "I do not
think that doubts respecting the facts related in the Gos-
pels need give us much trouble," he wrote his sister in

14. In an unusually long and didactic letter, Clough, only seventeen,
explained to his sister Annie the evils which an Established Church could
prevent, both in America and England. He began, "It is indeed a sad
mark of what the want of an Established Church will produce, that the
descendants of men like the old settlers in New England and Pennsylvania
and indeed all America should be so changed from the sincere and high-
minded zeal and piety of their fathers." Then he continues with what
amounts to a regular sermon, the flavor of which can be appreciated only
from reading the whole. (*Corr.*, I, 33)

1847. "Believing that in one way or other the thing is of God, we shall in the end know perhaps in what way and how far it was so." (*Corr.*, I, 182; *PPR*, I, 110–111) And later, in *Notes on the Religious Tradition*, he reiterated the rejection of the merely destructive criticism:

> I do not see that it is a great and noble thing, a needful or very worthy service, to go about proclaiming that Mark is inconsistent with Luke, that the first Gospel is not really Matthew's. . . . It is at the utmost a commendable piece of honesty.
>
> (*SPW*, p. 290; *PPR*, I, 422)

Clough took the position that the higher criticism could actually help strengthen man's spiritual faith by clearing away all unnecessary dogma and ritual, thus revealing its basic truths. Dr. Arnold had always warned against a strictly literal interpretation of Biblical events; and in his preface to *Leben Jesu*, Strauss had written: "The author is aware that the essence of the Christian faith is perfectly independent of his criticism. The supernatural birth of Christ, his miracles, his resurrection and ascension, remain eternal truths, whatever doubts may be cast on their reality as historical facts." [15] Joseph Beatty, Jr., pointing out the similarity between Strauss's view and that of Clough, wrote that Clough became "aware of discrepancies between the findings of science and the sacred books of the Hebrews," but that unlike the "more shallow thinkers of his day," Clough saw "beneath the surface of disputed texts and poetical interpretations a bedrock of spiritual

---

15. David F. Strauss, *The Life of Jesus,* tr. George Eliot, with an introduction by Otto Pfleiderer, London, 1906, p. xxx.

truth." [16] It was this "bedrock" that enabled Clough never to lose hope in Christianity; it was this same faith, together with his positive naturalism, that prevented him from becoming the complete skeptic or the complete mystic.

Clough's religion, then, cannot be regarded as a mark of his timid clinging to orthodox belief because he feared he would become an agnostic; his Christianity is not a "half-held creed," but one that identifies him as one of the enlightened thinkers of his time. His view of Christianity was a positive affirmation of faith, made only after he had carefully considered the evidence, and his mature position is characterized by an overwhelming desire to be free from spiritual despotism of any kind and a strong wish to base his conclusions on knowledge rather than on ignorance, on reasonableness rather than on fear or emotion. In the *Amours* he emphasized that "Knowledge is hard to seek, and harder yet to adhere to," although he would not agree with Claude that faith and love pass away. From America he wrote to his fiancée, "Energy is a very ordinary thing; reasonableness is much less common—and does ten times the good." (*Corr.*, II, 446; *PPR*, I, 207) Because of these views, he felt that the recognition of the historical doubts concerning Christianity was a badly needed step in the right direction; for it was only the attempt to reconcile the apparently irreconcilable contradictions present in the history of Christianity that had led many Christians to become either vague mystics or dogmatic philistines. If one were to ignore scientific and historical evidence, he would have to do so only by indulging in excessive mysticism or

16. Joseph M. Beatty, Jr., "Arthur Hugh Clough as Revealed in His Prose," *South Atlantic Quarterly*, XXV (April, 1926), 175.

devotionalism, as the Roman Catholics were prone to do, or in "enthusiasm" or blind benevolences, as the Protestant Evangelicals tended to do.[17]

His disapproval of the Catholic Church was due in large part to its excessive mysticism, which seemed to him a way to avoid facing facts. To him, mysticism was "letting feeling run on, without thinking of the reality of their object—letting it out merely like water," (*Corr.*, II, 398; *PPR*, I, 200) and his own commentary on the mystic response was expressed with clarity and force: "The plain rule in all matters is, not to think what you are thinking about the question, but to look straight out at the things and let them affect you; otherwise how can you judge at all? look at them at any rate, and judge while looking." (*PPR*, I, 200)

In addition to his aversion to their mysticism, Clough also could not countenance the Catholic emphasis on ritualism and devotionality. His long poem *Amours* contains some of his harshest pronouncements against these excesses, as time and time again Claude tells his friend

17. It is perhaps necessary to stress Clough's early sloughing off any Evangelical influences, since critics have attempted to make much of these. Indicative of Clough's attitude from the days at Rugby is a letter to his friend Simpkinson, part of which is printed in *Corr.*, I, 34–36. One of the omitted sections of this letter, dated 18 January, 1836, contains Clough's diagnosis of his schoolmate Fox: "He is disagreeable sometimes, particularly by continual talking in at lesson, and is rather narrow-minded or rather narrow-notioned. . . . It is this very narrowness of ideas that prevents one loving him. I know his home-people are very Evangelical, and such people have no idea that it is anything approaching to a duty to make oneself agreeable. They have a great deal too much of the itch to become martyrs and undergo persecution. Even 2 or 3 years under Arnold have not wholly eradicated this notion in Fox himself, but if he goes as I believe he does to Balliol, he will, I trust, lose it, as I think he is sure to be admitted into the High Arnold set that is just germinating at Balliol under the auspices of Stanley and Lake." (MSS, letter 31, Clough to Simpkinson)

how far from being really religious is the "holy city" and
the religion that it contains:

> *No, the Christian faith, as at any rate I understood it,*
> *With its humiliations and exaltations combining,*
> *Exaltations sublime, and yet diviner abasements,*
> *Aspirations from something most shameful here upon*
>   *earth and*
> *In our poor selves to something most perfect above in*
>   *the heavens,—*
> *No, the Christian faith, as I, at least, understood it,*
> *Is not here, O Rome, in any of these thy churches;*
> *Is not here, but in Freiburg, or Rheims, or Westminster*
>   *Abbey.*
>
> (*Poems,* p. 179)

He accuses the "vile, tyrannous Spaniards" of being responsible for these pernicious practices:

> *These are here still,—how long, O ye heavens, in the*
>   *country of Dante?*
> *These, that fanaticized Europe, which now can forget*
>   *them, release not*
> *This, their choicest of prey, this Italy; here you see*
>   *them,—*
> *Here, with emasculate pupils and gimcrack churches of*
>   *Gesu,*
> *Pseudo-learning and lies, confessional-boxes and pos-*
>   *tures,—*
> *Here, with metallic beliefs and regimental devotions,—*
> *Here, overcrusting with slime, perverting, defacing, de-*
>   *basing,*
> *Michael Angelo's dome, that had hung the Pantheon in*
>   *heaven,*
> *Raphael's Joys and Graces, and thy clear stars, Galileo!*
>
> (*Poems,* p. 180)

He continued his attack in his review of Newman's *The Soul:* "The belief that religion is or in any way requires devotionality," he wrote, "is if not the most noxious at least the most obstinate form of *ir*religion. . . . If we needs must classify the results of this spiritual misconception—and give a list at least of the forms of the evil first we must mention and dismiss that of pure devotionality, more common in Roman Catholic countries than in England. Here the religionist simply ignores the exterior world—all that is done is merely mechanical—absorption in the contemplation of the Deity is the whole life." (*SPW*, p. 282; *PPR*, I, 299)

But Clough was by no means only anti-Catholic; the Protestants were not entirely innocent. If excessive devotionality and ritualism that lead one to ignore reality were the failings of the Catholics, then failure to see facts was the main spiritual fault of the Protestants. Faced with the question of reconciling "the world and the Spirit," Clough states, some people, "stimulated by vague enthusiasm and tortured by over [-] irritable conscience . . . begin by accepting as the promptings of the Spirit any random suggestion of the fancy—if it occurs [to] them to write a letter to an irreligious relation, it must be done; . . . if a text turns up in their mind, it must be applied forthwith after a course of which sad mistakings—distressed by their uninstructed enthusiasm, yet baffled by defeats, and obliged to foresee evil consequence they end perhaps by leaving the decision to the turning of a piece of money, and find the spirit of wisdom in the head or tail of an appointed providential sixpence." (*SPW*, p. 283; *PPR*, I, 300)

If not indulging in "vague enthusiasm," Protestants were too often prone to still another religious failing:

"blind benevolence and alms-giving." Referring directly
to Protestantism in England, he wrote: "The more enlightened philanthropism of England resorts to . . .
formation of charitable societies—to district visiting, distribution of tracts, and teaching in charity Schools. . . .
It is to be feared that to many of the teachers, advisers,
and visitors occurs more or less frequently and sadly the
question What is it I shall say. As my own religion consists in praying, hearing sermons, and visiting the poor,
so that which I am to teach consists in praying, hearing
sermons, and . . . . . [sic] resignation to poverty!"
(*SPW*, pp. 283–284; *PPR*, I, 301)

Both Catholic and Protestant practices, then, because
they fail to relate man to the actual world, fail to satisfy
wholly the spiritual longing of man. For Clough, the result is tragic:

> And now . . . ask yourself this question!—At the end
> of your religious exercise and devotional indulgence, re-
> turning from prayer meetings and sacraments, and rising
> from the knees that bend in the closet to the Father that
> seëth in secret—at the end of all this what remains? An
> earnest desire to serve him, to do his Will [,] to do good:
> a desire and is it not true, a question, What shall I
> do?—This question, O reader, does it always find its
> answer and end where it found its beginning? . . . Do
> you not end ere . . . next prayer meeting or sacrament
> with a sense which that excitement alone can dispel, that
> after all [,] religion is in daily life sadly impracticable.
> . . . Your religious experience will indeed have been idle
> if you now resort again to your old Evangelicalisms; or
> fix yourself in simple devotionality if all this end in
> unmeaning oscillation, or stupid immobility.
>   (*SPW*, pp. 284–285; *PPR*, I, 303–304)

The great gap between religion and life was the heart of the problem. Religious experience of all types seemed to prove that religion was "sadly impracticable" in daily life, and people ended in "unmeaning oscillation" or "stupid immobility." Clough's constant satiric references to the conventional religious practices and beliefs of his time do not indicate that he himself could never resolve his own doubts; they mean simply that Clough recognized clearly the real divorce between life and religion in his time, and that he was doing all he could to shake his contemporaries out of an attitude towards religion that seemed to stress form and custom over real understanding.

The predicament was a familiar one to Clough, for he had seen his close friends struggling with it. Both Shairp and Theodore Walrond had appealed to him for advice at the time they were considering their future careers. In August, 1846, when he was having difficulty deciding whether to become ordained or not, Shairp indicated his specific dilemma:

The thing that offends one is that both in one's self and in most "good books" and perhaps some good people too the transition from positive Christianity to one's everyday feelings is so abrupt—on the one side is all you know and think about in a common way—on the other all you profess to believe. No attempt at bringing them into unity—unless in the case of those who take themselves to monasteries and this every-one sees to be unreal for most people. You will understand the disadjustment I mean. The difficulty arises from one's inability to pass off from a holding of certain facts into pure spiritual morality. Yet one sees it is necessary to hold to the facts for many reasons. . . . But as I said some [-] how or

other the facts and the truths behind them have got dis-
adjusted and who will put them right?

(MSS, letter 229, August 26)

A few weeks later he wrote again: "I think the difficulty is
that in the dogma of an historical Saviour and redemption there is something of positive and arbitrary cruel[ty]
which does not blend with the truths of morality. So that
in the pulpit men talk of the dogma—in practice they
hold to conscience and themselves never pass one into the
other. All this would seem unreal." (MSS, letter 232,
September 12 or 19)

Walrond, too, thought Clough could counsel him, and in
August, 1847, he asked Clough's opinion on the subject of
a career, which he had been discussing with his father. Of
particular interest are his comments on the clergy, which
seemed one of the few professions left to him:

I think I shall very likely come back to orders :—not with
the same feelings which made me look upon it as the only
profession for an earnest man: but as a simple straight
forward [sic] way of doing good (making money the
while) :—and I do not think it would be necessary for me
to falsify my nature, either on the one hand or on the
other, to become a good clergyman. I mean I should not,
I hope, have to turn half-hypocrite, as many men do, to
whom an atmosphere of habitual and professional piety
is altogether unnatural—though I know it is not entirely
natural to me: nor have I any of those larger and freer
views and feelings which both you and Shairp have,
which would be violated by becoming a minister of the
Church of England.

(MSS, letter 257, August; Chorley, p. 116)

Everywhere in Clough's later works, particularly in his shorter satires and the long one *Dipsychus,* is evident his desire to heal this "disadjustment" of facts and truths so characteristic of Christianity. His satire is discussed in greater detail below, but at this point his concern over religious practices is clearly revealed by various ideas expressed in the satiric writings of this period. In "The Latest Decalogue" he strikes directly at those who look upon their religion as a comfortable convention, necessary to their being well thought of by their friends and acquaintances:

> *Thou shalt have one God only; who*
> *Would be at the expense of two?*
> *No graven images may be*
> *Worshipped, except the currency:*
> *Swear not at all; for for thy curse*
> *Thine enemy is none the worse:*
> *At church on Sunday to attend*
> *Will serve to keep the world thy friend:*
>
>   *   *   *
>
> *Thou shalt not steal; an empty feat,*
> *When it's so lucrative to cheat:*
>
>   *   *   *
>
> *Thou shalt not covet; but tradition*
> *Approves all forms of competition.*
>
>   (*Poems,* pp. 60–61)

The same condemnation is found in other poems written at this time. In "I dreamed a dream: I dreamt that I espied," an unfinished poem dealing with the return of Christ as a "shade" and his disturbing effect on the people who have accepted conventional religion, one of the figures, the "World," expresses his fears about the trouble

that the returned Christ might cause. He insists that the
old order and peace must be preserved:

> *His wife and daughter must have where to pray,*
> *And whom to pray to, at the least one day*
> *In seven, and something definite to say.*
> *Whether the fact so many years ago*
> *Had, or not, happened, how was he to know?*
> *Yet he had always heard that it was so.*
> *As for himself, perhaps it was all one;*
> *And yet he found it not unpleasant, too,*
> *On Sunday morning in the roomy pew,*
> *To see the thing with such decorum done.*
> *As for himself, perhaps it was all one;*
> *Yet on one's death-bed all men always said*
> *It was a comfortable thing to think upon*
> *The Atonement and the Resurrection of the dead.*
> *So the great World as having said his say,*
> *Unto his country-house pursued his way.*

The Pope too is disturbed:

> *And the poor Pope was sure it must be so,*
> *Else wherefore did the people kiss his toe?*
> *The subtle Jesuit cardinal shook his head,*
> *And mildly looked and said,*
> *It mattered not a jot*
> *Whether the thing, indeed, were so or not;*
> *Religion must be kept up, and the Church preserved,*
> *And for the people this best served.*

The dignitaries of the Church are disturbed about the possible loss of revenue:

> *And dignitaries of the Church came by.*
> *It had been worth to some of them, they said,*
> *Some £100,000 a year a head.*

> *If it fetched so much in the market, truly,*
> *'Twas not a thing to be given up unduly.*
> (*Poems*, pp. 407–408)

Strictures on meaningless religion are also scattered through *Dipsychus*, but Clough's disgust with conventional or routine religion probably reaches its height in the scene at the Academy. Dipsychus, beginning to tire of inaction and fruitless thinking, decides to find out the terms of surrender to the Spirit. "Religion goes, I take it," he tells the Spirit; but the Spirit surprises and shocks him. Of course Dipsychus will not have to give up religion; on the contrary, he must keep up his churchly duties and attendance. The religious way of the world must be maintained. As a matter of fact, says the Spirit, it would be well if Dipsychus would enter holy orders, for, after all, that is not a bad way to make a living. (*Poems*, p. 267)

Perhaps the only other section in the poem where Clough's satire is as powerful is that in which the Spirit advises Dipsychus to stop all this needless hair-splitting over matters of religion and adopt the "proper" point of view:

> *Take larger views (and quit your Germans)*
> *From the Analogy and Sermons;*
> *I fancied—you must doubtless know—*
> *Butler had proved, an age ago,*
> *That in religious as profane things*
> *'Twas useless trying to explain things;*
> *Men's business-wits the only sane things,*
> *These and compliance are the main things.*
>   *   *   *
> *Like a good subject and wise man,*
> *Believe whatever things you can.*

> *Take your religion as 'twas found you,*
> *And say no more of it—confound you!*
> (*Poems*, pp. 264–265)

In his own Christianity, his "true creed," Clough, refusing to take his religion as 'twas found him, wanted more than routine conventions. First, recognizing clearly the significance of the higher criticism, he acknowledged the historical doubts connected with the Christian religion. In 1852 he wrote to his cousin Margaret Clough that, although he felt free to say that he thought the Christian religion the best or "perhaps only really good religion that has appeared," he felt that there were many possible doubts as to how it appeared. "The whole origin of Xty is lost in uncertainty," he concluded. (*Corr.*, I, 304–305; *PPR*, I, 171–172) In his *Notes on the Religious Tradition* he wrote that it was impossible for any scholar to have read, studied, and reflected without forming a strong impression "of the entire uncertainty of history in general— and of the history of the origin of Christianity in particular. . . . Manuscripts are doubtful, records may be unauthentic, criticism is feeble, historical facts must be left uncertain.—" (*SPW*, p. 289; *PPR*, I, 421)

But the uncertainty of historical facts did not disturb him; he saw that beneath these contradictions lay that bedrock of spiritual truth that would sustain man. For Clough, at least, it was impossible for any man "to live, act, and reflect without feeling the significance and depth of the moral and religious teaching which passes amongst us by the name of Christianity." (*PPR*, I, 421; see also *Corr.*, I, 304) However, in order to feel this significance and depth, man had to learn to separate accessories from essentials: "It is conceivable [he wrote in the *Notes*] that religious truths of the highest import may grow up naturally, and appear before us involved in uncertain traditions, with every sort of mere accessory legend and story attached to them and entangled with them." (*SPW*, p. 291; *PPR*, I, 423)

Clough, of course, did learn to separate the essential truth from the accessories, and he became more concerned with the philosophic ideas and the symbolic truths to be gained from Christianity rather than with its historical or scientific accuracy. "The thing which men must work at," he told his sister in 1847, "will not be critical questions about the scriptures, but philosophical problems of Grace and Free Will, and of Redemption as an Idea, not as an historical event." [18] In the *Notes* he reiterated this idea. "It may be true," he wrote, "that as the physical bread has to be digested, and the nutritive portion separated from the innutritive, so may it also be with the Spiritual.—" (*SPW*, p. 291; *PPR*, I, 423) He is willing to accept the events in the Bible as symbolic rather than literal truths: "Whether Christ died upon the Cross, I cannot tell; yet I am prepared to find some spiritual truth in

18. *Corr.*, I, 182; *PPR,* I, 111. Other specific comments are recorded in the *Memoir*. In 1845, discussing the subject of baptism with his sister, he told her that he was inclined to regard it as "merely a sort of form which had been instituted as a sign of admission into the early Christian Church, and useful then, when outward signs for everything were constantly required," but that he was now inclined to "doubt whether there was any use in continuing it." (p. 56) In April of 1846 he made an even more significant statement in a discussion with Conybeare. "Arthur thought," his sister wrote, "it was a great duty to destroy or explain any dogmas or doctrines that might stand in the way of these unbelievers becoming Christians, and to show them that Christianity was what they wanted to make them perfect." (p. 60)

the Doctrine of the Atonement. Purgatory is not in the Bible; I do not therefore think it incredible.—" (*SPW*, p. 292; *PPR*, I, 425)

The knowledge that Clough did find a creed in which he could believe with heart and mind enables us to see in a new light two of his most moving poems, "*Epi-Strauss-ium*" and "Easter Day," I and II. Since they are central documents in the religious thinking of Clough, both poems must be given a great deal more emphasis than they have had up to now. Both are poetic utterances of his "new creed." In "*Epi-Strauss-ium*," written in 1847, just one year before he left Oxford, we find stated poetically what he had been saying in his letters and what he was to emphasize in his later essays and poetry: the value of the higher criticism and his faith in a "bedrock of spiritual truth." Certainly the image of the sunlight coming through "windows plainly glassed," making the place of worship "more sincerely bright," could not have been written by one who, in the words of one critic, resigned himself when he resigned from Oxford. On the contrary, the poem is a statement of faith and hope in the "true creed."

In the same way, "Easter Day" needs to be re-examined, especially the relationship of the two parts. The pessimism of the first part is often cited as proof of Clough's overwhelming grief at the loss of all his orthodox beliefs and as evidence of the doubt that critics claim overwhelmed him the rest of his life. If the second part is mentioned at all, it is usually cited as a half-hearted attempt, and an unsuccessful one, to offset the pessimism of the first. Actually, however, the poem is Clough's most passionate statement of his positive attitude towards Christianity. From this point of view, the first part is not pessimistic; it is

Clough's rejection of the obstacles that have stood in the way of his wholehearted acceptance of Christianity: the necessity of having to believe in the historical truth of Christ, His actual existence, His resurrection, and all the supernatural events connected with Him. Part I is Clough's statement that "the whole origin of Christianity is lost in obscurity." Part II is his statement of acceptance of the symbolic truths of Christianity. Even though we cannot believe in the historical truths of Christianity, we should, he states, believe in the "essence" of the Christian message, the basic beliefs upon which Christianity was originally founded.

The two parts of the poem, then, are not contrasts in pessimism and optimism, but complementary contributions to a positive religious approach. The rejection of the accessories of Christianity in Part I:

> *What though the stone were rolled away, and though*
> * The grave found empty there!—*
> * If not there, then elsewhere;*
> *If not where Joseph laid Him first, why then*
> * Where other men*
> *Translaid Him after; in some humbler clay*
> * Long ere to-day*
> *Corruption that sad perfect work hath done,*
> *Which here she scarcely, lightly had begun.*
> * The foul engendered worm*
> *Feeds on the flesh of the life-giving form*
> *Of our most Holy and Anointed One.*
>
> * He is not risen, no,*
> * He lies and moulders low;*
> *   Christ is not risen.*

(Poems, pp. 54–55)

is replaced by the inward assurance of the "true creed" in the second part:

> *But in a later hour I sat and heard*
> *Another voice that spake, another graver word.*
> *Weep not, it bade, whatever hath been said,*
> *Though He be dead, He is not dead.*
> *In the true Creed*
> *He is yet risen indeed,*
> *Christ is yet risen.*
>
> * * *
>
> *Though dead, not dead;*
> *Not gone, though fled;*
> *Not lost, not vanished.*
> *In the great Gospel and true Creed,*
> *He is yet risen indeed;*
> *Christ is yet risen.*
>
> (*Poems*, pp. 59–60)

From the tone of quiet but intense self-confidence that permeates this second part, we are able to see that Clough had seen through all the incrustation that had formed about Christianity; he had indeed caught a clear glimpse of its soul.

Besides this strong faith in an unnameable Deity and a sincere belief in the "essence" of Christianity, Clough's religious position was marked by his unshakeable confidence in duty as service to one's fellow man, an idea based firmly, of course, on his positive naturalism. Once he came to the point of accepting human nature for what it was, with both its pleasant and unpleasant characteristics, his emphasis was on the need to stop theorizing about abstract questions and to turn to the world and make the best of it, principally by serving man. Determined to avoid mysticism, ritualism, or mere formalism, he felt that this concept of duty served to bring religion out of the theoretical into the practical stage. Many critics, in attempting to give an explanation for Clough's so-called failure, stress his constant search for truth and his apparent despair at not finding it during his lifetime. They fail to see, first of all, that Clough looked upon truth not as a pure abstraction but as a synonym for God, and, secondly, that he, like Dr. Arnold, came to look upon truth as the ultimate and service as the immediate goal in this life. The same words that Matthew Arnold said about his father could well be said of Clough: "For him . . . conduct was three-fourths of [life]—probably more." Or, as Martha Hale Schackford has put it: "By every implication Clough asserts his belief in a sort of Pragmatism." [19]

Even while at Oxford Clough had come to look upon duty as the one way to make religion meaningful in one's life. Subjected on all sides to different theories and doctrines, he emerged from this experience with the strong belief that man's ultimate salvation lay in his turning away from needless wrangling over abstractions and, instead, helping his fellow man as best he could. Service became for him in the religious sphere, as well as in the social one, the concrete expression of man's worship of God. Instead of trying to count the number of angels on the head of a pin, man should do his utmost to serve others; this belief is the core of Clough's "Everlasting Yea" and a valuable guide to the interpretation of many of his poems, essays, and acts.

The ultimate justification for Clough's belief in service

19. Martha Hale Shackford, "The Clough Centenary: His *Dipsychus*," *Sewanee Review*, XXVII (October, 1919), 406.

lies in the quality which I have referred to up to now as his
positive naturalism, the chief marks of which are the acceptance of human nature for what it is and the belief in
the native goodness of man. So important was this to
Clough that it affected not only his religious thinking but
his entire outlook towards life itself, and, for this reason,
it is important that we understand completely what this
idea implies. I have already suggested some of its implications in the Introduction, but perhaps the clearest
statement is that by Trilling in his discussion of how it
concerns E. M. Forster, to whom I have earlier likened
Clough in this one respect. "Most of us," writes Trilling,
"consciously or unconsciously, are discontented with the
nature rather than with the use of the human faculty; deep
in our assumption lies the hope and the belief that humanity will end its career by developing virtues which will be
admirable exactly because we cannot now conceive them.
. . . This is a moral and historical error into which Forster never falls; his whole work . . . is an implied protest
against it. . . . The way of human action of course does
not satisfy him, but he does not believe there are any new
virtues to be discovered; not by becoming better, he says,
but by ordering and distributing his native goodness can
man live as befits him." (Trilling, pp. 22–23) Clough, too,
did not fall into this moral and historical failure. He too
was dissatisfied with human action. He too came to center
his attention not on the nature of but on the use of the human faculty. He too came, as did Forster, to accept "the
human fact as we know it now." (Trilling, p. 22) Clough's
attitude in all this was positive rather than negative, optimistic rather than pessimistic, and it explains the practical
innocence and the moral realism that characterize both his

life and work. "People," he told his fiancée just before his
departure for America in 1852, "should not be *very* scep-
tical about things in general. . . . There are plenty of
good things in the world, and good persons. Fitness is a
great deal, but truth is a great deal more. If things are
good, we ought to accept them as such; looking at *them*,
and not thinking of our own fitness." (*PPR*, I, 178) Another time he told her: "I . . . have always been inclined
to believe in the good of the world;—have always acted on
that belief except for a brief interval (just when you knew
me) and even then it was partly that I was afraid lest I
should be trusting my own vague hopefulness too unrea-
sonably." (*Corr.*, II, 371; *PPR*, I, 195)

Once Clough's positive naturalism, his acceptance of
the goodness of things and people, is understood, then his
idea of duty as service takes on a positive quality that has
been disregarded up to now. It is, obviously, his attempt
to make religion meaningful in one's life. Critics have
tended to regard Clough's emphasis on doing one's duty
while waiting for the "heavenly light" as either a weak
imitation of the Carlylean doctrine of work as prayer or
as proof of his negative view of life, wherein he is content
merely to wait and never do. They have tended to emphasize his plea for waiting rather than his plea for serving
one's fellow man while waiting. But Clough himself emphasized the service, not the waiting, and this emphasis is
evident in all his writing, as well as his own life. In one of
his early poems, "I have seen higher holier things than
these," the emphasis is on the doing:

> *The* Summum Pulchrum *rests in heaven above;*
> *Do thou, as best thou may'st, thy duty do:*

> *Amid the things allowed thee live and love;*
> *Some day thou shalt it view.*
>
> (Poems, p. 34)

Clough also has Adam say in the *Bothie*, written just after he left Oxford, "We have all something to do, man, woman alike, I own it;/ We have all something to do, and in my judgment should do it." And the work that Clough advocates in the *Bothie* is work like teaching and nursing, occupations that stress service to others. In *Dipsychus* he is even more specific regarding that which is more important, the doing or the waiting: "It seems His newer will/ We should not think of Him at all, but trudge it,/ And of the world He has assigned us make/ What best we can."

The necessity of positive action, especially that of service to others, is also the theme of other poems, poems seldom cited by those who would stress Clough's waiting rather than doing. In "Hope evermore and believe, O man" (1850), there is an exhortation to duty: "Not for the gain of the gold, for the getting, the hoarding, the having,/ But for the joy of the deed; but for the Duty to do." (*Poems*, p. 63) In "Last Words. Napoleon and Wellington" (1853), Clough commends Wellington for his recognition that duty and service are all-important:

> *Not stirring words, nor gallant deeds alone,*
> *Plain patient work fulfilled that length of life;*
> *Duty, not glory—Service, not a throne,*
> *Inspired his effort, set for him the strife.*
>
> (Poems, p. 94)

The stress on doing is carried into his latest poetry, his *Mari Magno or Tales on Board*, all of which, significantly, deal with the practical problems connected with love and

marriage. In the "Lawyer's First Tale," Clough has a
married woman advise her younger cousin, who is thinking of remaining at college and becoming a don, to leave
the college and, instead, enter into the activities of life:

> *I know it will be just a crime*
> *If you should waste your powers and time.*
> *There is so much, I think, that you,*
> *And no one equally, can do.*
>
>   (*Poems*, p. 330)

The conscious effort to connect religion with daily living
is found in his essays and letters, as well as in his poetry.
"Enter the arena of your brethren," he wrote in 1850 to
J. C. Shairp, "and go not to your grave without knowing
what common merchants and sollicitors [sic], much more
sailors and coalheavers, are well acquainted with. Ignorance is a poor kind of innocence." (*Corr.*, I, 284; *PPR*,
I, 168) Three years later he wrote to his fiancée from
America: "the only way to become really religious is to
enter into those relations and those actualities of life which
demand and create religion." (*Corr.*, II, 392; *PPR*, I,
200) [20]

The clearest and most explicit statements regarding
Clough's deep-seated conviction that religion must be tied
in with the actualities of life are found in the two documents that deal specifically with religion, his review of
The Soul and the *Notes*. In the review his stress on serving

20. His emphasis on being concerned with the actualities of life is
also evident in his poetic theory, for he insisted that poetry, too, deal
more than it presently did in his time with "general wants, ordinary feelings, the obvious rather than the rare facts of human nature," and his
Mari Magno tales deal mostly with practical problems of love and marriage. The very close connection of Clough's thought and art has up to
now been much too neglected.

God through serving others predominates. For Clough the answer to the question "What shall I do?" is clear:

> We are here, however we came, to do something . . . to serve God. The World is here, however it came here, to be made something of by our hands. Not by prayer, but examination; examination not of ourselves, but of the world, shall we find out what to do, and how to do it. Not by looking up into our Master's face shall we learn the meaning of the book which he has put into our hands. . . . We have said, Look not up into the empty airs, but upon the solid, somewhat dirty Earth around underfoot.
>
> (*SPW*, pp. 285–286; *PPR*, I, 304–305)

In his *Notes* there is an even greater emphasis on the necessity for the person who would be truly religious to turn to the world. In his own words, all religious values, particularly the "essential truths" of Christianity, are to be found "Everywhere.—But above all in our own work, in life, in action, in submission so far as action goes[,] in service—in experience—in patience and in confidence." (*SPW*, p. 291; *PPR*, I, 424)

To those who regard religion in the orthodox sense of narrow creeds, established hierarchies, and rigid codes, this practical, all-embracing, "natural" religion of Clough's, with its emphasis on social rather than theological morality, may seem to be no religion at all; and perhaps that is the reason he has become the symbolic figure of the Victorian doubter. But Clough's religion must not be judged by these standards. The truth is that Clough did achieve a religious philosophy that was for him practically useful and deeply satisfying, for religion to him became not only a creed but a way of life. And just as his writings take on new meaning when his religious position becomes more fully known, so do certain actions that he took. His resignation from Oxford, his being asked to resign from University Hall, his work for the Education Office, and his great pleasure in working for Florence Nightingale were all due to his religious beliefs. It can be said of him as of few others that he practiced his religion, the best illustrations being his work at the Education Office and his important, if not especially glamorous, efforts in behalf of Florence Nightingale.

His duties in the Education Office began in July, 1853, and continued until 1859, when ill health forced him to leave. Many of his duties consisted of detailed work, such as revising grades and reviewing reports, but he seldom complained of this "quill-driving," for he felt that by this work he was doing his own small part in serving others. It is true, of course, that he accepted this position because of the financial security it offered; but it is also important to remember that Clough saw in education an important and necessary process of life, one that had done a great deal of good for England and the world. His faith in education had enabled him early in his Oxford career to feel justified in signing the Thirty-nine Articles:

> I can feel faith [he had written to J. P. Gell] in what is being carried on by my generation and . . . I am content to be an operative—to dress intellectual leather, cut it out to pattern and stitch it and cobble it into boots and shoes for the benefit of the work which is being guided by wiser heads.
>
> (*Corr.*, I, 140 ; *PPR*, I, 95)

He was able to carry on his duties in the Education Office with a quiet certainty of their value; they unquestionably constituted that service to his fellow man demanded by his religious beliefs.

His work with Florence Nightingale was even more compatible with his religious principles. Clough, who met Miss Nightingale through Blanche, sincerely admired her and became devoted to her service. She, in turn, fretted over him in her own peculiar and domineering way. When Clough met her, she was just beginning her famous career in nursing, and he spent every possible spare moment helping her. When she and her party of nurses left London on October 21, 1854, for the Crimea, Clough went to Calais to see them off. He continued his help in various ways until his death, revising her work, correcting proof, arranging schedules, delivering reports; for a time he was Secretary to the Nightingale Fund. There have been critics, particularly those after Lytton Strachey, who have made sarcastic or pitying remarks concerning Clough's work for Miss Nightingale. Observing Clough from the outside, failing to understand his basic viewpoint, they have naturally been unable to find the clue to Clough's devoted interest in this work; they have regarded it merely as the desperate effort of a "halting, timid, over-patient man" to keep busy and save himself from the slough of despondency. The clue to Clough's concern for this work lies in his belief of service; he saw an opportunity to do his "humble, simple duty" in such a way that it would benefit many people, and he made the most of it.

Sir Edward Cook writes that Clough did his work for Miss Nightingale with "cheerful modesty," and that he was intent upon "doing plain work." And Miss Nightingale herself, one of the few people who really understood this aspect of Clough's thought, realized the satisfaction that he received from doing this. She wrote in one of her letters: "My idea of a friend is one who will and can join you in work the sole purpose of which is to serve God. Two in one, and one in God. It almost exactly answers Jesus Christ's words. And so extraordinarily blessed have I been that I have had three such friends." [21] Clough, of course, was one of these, and Florence Nightingale exactly understood his purpose in helping her. Here was some practical duty that was of help to mankind, and Clough was delighted to play a part in the cause, no matter how small it was.

A. McKinley Terhune is correct, then, in stating that the greatest riddle to confront Clough was that reflected in his struggle between faith and doubt.[22] But Clough found the answer to this riddle, and the failure of the critics to recognize this has resulted in a great deal of misunderstanding of his life and writing, his thought and art. When his religious position—consisting of a belief in God, a belief in the essence of Christianity, a belief in the necessary connection between theory and practice, and a belief in the native goodness of man and the world—is seen in clear perspective, many of his essays, letters, poems, and acts take on new meaning. "It fortifies my soul to know" is no longer a "stoical understatement," but a poem in praise of God; "Easter Day," II, is not a half-hearted attempt to offset "Easter Day," I, but a confident expres-

21. Sir Edward Cook, *The Life of Florence Nightingale*, 2 vols., London, 1913, II, 222–223.
22. A. McKinley Terhune, "Arthur Hugh Clough," *The Victorian Poets: A Guide to Research*, ed. F. E. Faverty, Cambridge, Mass., 1956, p. 108.

sion of his faith in the essential truths of Christianity. And his work in the Education Office and for Florence Nightingale is not drifting, but a positive effort to connect religion and life, a concrete expression of his positive naturalism. The recognition of Clough's positive religious faith will go a long way towards establishing the vital connection between his thought and art and indicating his significant contribution to Victorian literature.

(B) The political and social position

Clough's religious position, with its great emphasis on service, is very closely related to his social, political, and economic thought; but again, as with his religious thought, few attempts have been made to establish clearly his specific ideas on and conclusions about the social and political events of his time. And this failure to understand his ideas in these areas has created the same difficulties brought about by the failure to understand his religious ideas, particularly concerning his life, thought, and art. It has, for instance, brought about the misunderstanding of the relationship between Clough and such figures as Dr. Arnold and Thomas Carlyle; it has led to the misinterpretation of many of his poems and acts; and, most seriously perhaps, it has denied him credit for the positive nature of his thoughts in these areas.

Perhaps the area in which this failure has been most harmful to Clough's reputation is that of his poetry, for the frequent misreadings of such poems as the *Bothie* and, especially, *Dipsychus* have resulted from a failure to understand exactly what Clough was saying about man's role on this "somewhat dirty earth" on which he lived. Unable to see Clough's positive naturalism in the social context, critics have been unable to make a distinction between "submission" as they see it and as Clough was able to see it. This particular matter will be discussed more fully below, however; at this point a more obvious example that demonstrates the misinterpretations that arise because of the failure to understand what Clough was thinking may be seen in the critical treatment of Clough's relationship with Carlyle. Critics, attempting to solve what has now become known as the "Clough enigma," have examined the friendship between the two men and most of them have concluded that Carlyle had a harmful effect on his younger friend.

Taking their cue from the famous anecdote of Clough's telling Emerson that "Carlyle led us out into the wilderness and left us there," many critics have attempted to demonstrate that Clough's intellectual, as well as spiritual, "failure" was due in large measure to his unsuccessful attempt to live his life according to the Carlylean gospel. The tenor of this criticism is illustrated by Osborne, who writes that one can best understand Clough's "singular inaction" during his years at Oxford by "seeing that he was proposing to be himself a Great Silent Man, and that while he appeared to be doing nothing, he was in fact sedulously ridding his spirit of its Old Clothes, and preparing himself, *alas, in vain* [italics mine], for the pealing through all the recesses of his being of his own 'Everlasting Yea.'" (p. 65)

There are a number of implications in this criticism that need to be more thoroughly investigated. First, this criti-

cism assumes that Clough never achieved his own "Everlasting Yea," an assumption by no means proved. Second,
this criticism asserts that Carlyle's influence was an inimical one, without which Clough would have been much
better off, intellectually and spiritually. To see him as a
frustrated Carlylean, as Osborne does, is to distort the
relationship between the two, mainly on the basis of misunderstanding Clough's thought. That Clough was deeply
influenced by Carlyle is undeniable; but rather than "re-
tard" Clough in his development (Osborne, p. 147), Carlyle's teachings had, it would seem, the opposite effect.
After Clough's orthodox opinions had been swept away, a
process to which Carlyle himself contributed, he did wander in the wilderness for a time; but the Carlylean concepts which had contributed to the sweeping away of
Clough's orthodox opinions helped also to provide a sub-
stantial base upon which to build new ones. To see the
Carlylean influence only as a negative one is to see only
one side of the coin. Carlyle may have led Clough into the
wilderness, but he was also responsible for helping him
find his way out.

As has been suggested, Clough's thought on religious
questions is closely connected to his thought on the social
ones; both areas reflect his primary concern with service to
mankind, which, in turn, is a reflection of his positive
naturalism or moral realism. In fact, the religious interpretation of service is the best explanation for Clough's
shift from speculation about to practical interest in contemporary social, political, and economic affairs. "When
he became unable to subscribe to the creeds of the church,"
Beatty writes, "it was an easy step for him to become interested in human welfare." (p. 177) This interest in

human welfare, in finding the way in which man could best put to use his native goodness, is most evident in Clough's concern in four particular areas of man's social, political, and economic activity: laissez-faire, property, the class structure, and labor. To understand his ideas in these areas is to gain an insight into his thought and life and a fuller appreciation of his art.

These four areas, of course, would be the major ones of interest to any intelligent, concerned, observant Victorian, since the age was marked by far-reaching social, political, and economic changes. The industrial revolution—spurred on by the reluctance of the government to initiate or to accept responsibility in social legislation, the Utilitarian philosophy of self-interest and concern for the greatest good for the greatest number, and the laissez-faire concept of non-interference in economic and industrial affairs that was creating a "cash-nexus" relationship between the middle-class capitalist and the laboring-class "hand"—had indeed made the age a "mechanistic" one. But to most Victorians, as they looked about them, the changes seemed to be for the better; progress seemed to have been made. The average Victorian had only to open his eyes, as did Thomas Babington Macaulay, spokesman for the belief in progress, to see that, in spite of slums and the denigration of the workers, all classes of the community were really better off than they had been in the past. Macaulay believed in progress, no matter what critics like Carlyle and others, including Clough, thought and said, because it was obvious that the average Englishman was far better off materially than he had ever been. Blind to the great evils that the machine had brought with it, Macaulay insisted on citing statistics:

In the first place, the poor-rate is very decidedly lower in the manufacturing than in the agricultural districts. . . . As to the effect of the manufacturing system on the bodily health, we must beg leave to estimate it by a standard far too low and vulgar for a mind so imaginative as that of Mr. Southey, the proportion of births and deaths. . . . There is the best reason to believe that the annual mortality of Manchester, about the middle of the last century, was one in twenty-eight. It is reckoned now at one in forty-five. . . . We might with some plausibility maintain that the people live longer because they are better fed, better lodged, better clothed, and better attended in sickness, and that these improvements are owing to that increase of national wealth which the manufacturing system has produced.[1]

Macaulay, of course, was speaking for the new order. The application of science to industry, begun in the late eighteenth century, had changed the entire face of the British nation, as well as its entire way of life. At the beginning of the period, England had been mainly an agricultural country; at the end, it was industrial, the workshop of the world. With the growth of industry, the change from handicrafts and domestic manufacture to machine-made goods and mass production, population and wealth had increased, and ugly manufacturing towns like Manchester, Sheffield, and Birmingham were created. Everywhere there was material progress. For fifty years of Victoria's reign, from 1837 to 1887, as one critic has remarked, "experts record fabulous increases in export and import trade and in national income, resulting . . . in increased wages and improved standards of living

1. Lord Macaulay, *Miscellaneous Works,* ed. by his sister Lady Trevelyan, 5 vols., New York, n. d., I, 402–403.

among the artisan classes, and in decreased pauperism and serious crime among the lowest classes." [2] Surely the idea of progress seemed justified.

The great flaw in the thinking of Macaulay and the average Victorian was that they confused progress with material advance; but Carlyle did not, and neither did Clough. How or why Macaulay and many Victorians failed to see the problems fostered by the machine age is a puzzle, for there was much evidence of the existence of these problems: political, social, and economic. The Corn Laws, for instance, were not repealed until the "hungry forties," an indication of the power of the aristocratic landowners in their opposition to the will of the people, who simply wanted enough bread to eat. In the political sphere, the small gains of the three Reform Bills of 1832, 1867, and 1885 showed the difficulties encountered by those who desired more local representation and more democratic practices. The Chartist fiasco of 1839 was a still more violent manifestation of these desires, and the apparently reasonable demand of the Chartists—representation by population, male suffrage, secret ballot, annual parliaments, and salaries for members of parliament—only served to accent the hardships suffered by the people of a nation being transformed from an aristocracy to a parliamentary democracy.

In the social and economic spheres, the situation was even worse; for with the creation of giant industrial cities were also born the problems of factory work and slum living, the existence of the laborers being characterized by one writer of the period as a "foul current of life running like a pestilential sewer beneath the smooth surface of

2. F. W. Roe, *Victorian Prose,* New York, 1947, p. xiii.

society." [3] Certainly the picture would not be an encourag-
ing one to an intelligent, sensitive person like Clough. For
a long time nearly naked women and children had been
forced to work from eleven to twelve hours a day in the
coal and iron mines. Child labor had also been the rule in
textile mills, and it was only with the Factory Act of 1833,
which limited the work of children under thirteen to an
eight-hour day and of children between thirteen and sixteen to a sixty-nine-hour week, that any reform could
become possible. Wages were on a starvation level, and
working conditions unbelievably poor, the Captains of Industry, the capitalistic factory owners, feeling that they
could do what they wished with their "hands." Unventi-
lated and unheated or overheated factories, unprotected
machinery, and monotonous work prevailed. The conditions of workers at home were not much better. Houses
were built along narrow, dark, dirty streets. Disease and
dirt were rampant; the mortality rate was incredibly high.
It was, as John Morley wrote, "a purgatory for the able,
and a hell for the poor."

Because of the reluctance of parliament to act and the
prevailing laissez-faire philosophy, help came slowly for
these wretched workers. Speaking of the workman in England, Clough had written to his friend Thomas Burbidge
in 1844, "I do believe that he has not his proper proportion, that capital tyrannizes over labour, and that government is bound to interfere to prevent such bullying."
(*Corr.*, I, 126–127; *PPR*, I, 91) And it was through legislation by the government that the worker's conditions were
improved, but the process was slow and gradual. The Factory Act of 1833 has already been mentioned. The Mines

3. A writer in the *Saturday Review*, 1865, cited by Roe, p. xv.

Act of 1842 was passed to restrict the employment of children to boys over nine and to prohibit the use of girls and
women underground. The Ten Hours Bill (1847) limited
the daily work of women and children in textile mills to ten
hours a day, a practice which gradually spread to other in-
dustries. In addition to these measures, trade unionism was
begining to gain relief for the workers. The Combination
Acts, which had outlawed unions, was repealed in 1825, and
the next decade saw a remarkable growth in trade unions,
the most ambitious being Robert Owen's famous Grand
National Consolidated. Owen's venture failed, but it and
others like it, together with legislative, political, and edu-
cational aid, led the way to the Conspiracy and Protection
of Property Act of 1875, which granted the unions the
right of peaceful picketing and thus paved the way to the
establishment of our modern unions.

The central problem in all these difficulties is, of course,
the problem of human beings, for the problem of man's
"happiness" and usefulness in life can be solved only on
the basis of how he is regarded and what his relationship
to his fellow men and to God is. In experiencing his own
spiritual and intellectual trials, Clough came to see that
the immediate problem for human beings here on earth was
not one of establishing a relationship with God through a
religious creed; it was, rather, one of first establishing a
satisfactory relationship with one's fellow man and of
finding one's own place in the society of which one was a
part. The great concern was the here and now, to do something with and make the best of the world assigned us by
God. In the light of these conclusions, he began to give
most of his attention to human affairs, particularly those
four areas mentioned above; and, as Palmer has pointed

out, his exploration of them was based on two principles that are perfectly natural in the light of his positive naturalism and his religious thought. He demonstrates, first, an "earnest sympathy with victims of oppression or poverty," and, second, a "desire for the triumph of genuine liberty." [4] To distinguish the genuine from the artificial was, of course, always Clough's principal aim.

Clough's religious ideas and his essentially sympathetic view of human nature are in direct contrast to both the spirit of commercialism and the philosophy of Utilitarianism that were such important influences in his time, and it is not surprising that he took an early interest in political economy and laissez-faire. Some of his student essays at Balliol (1837–1841) reveal his displeasure with bourgeoise materialism and selfish utilitarianism. In one essay (February 8, 1838) he wrote: "In our own age the Utilitarian view of philosophy may be regarded with probable truth as the offspring of the previous failure and abuse of higher principles." In another essay of 1839–1840 he went into some detail regarding the evils of commerce, particularly the "thirst for gain" and the "increase of luxury." "What wonder," he stated, "if the maxim of men's conduct should now become Seek money first and Virtue after: and if they themselves should be ready to sacrifice self-respect and affection, kindly feelings and noble impulses of all kinds in obedience to this new Principle." [5]

4. Palmer, "Was Clough a Failure?" p. 63.
5. MSS, "English Essays, 1837–1841." In *Checklist* these essays are listed on pp. 380–381; in *SPW*, on pp. 346–348. The essay for February 8, 1838, is number xiii for 1837–1838, "The Prevalence under Different Circumstances of Different Systems of Philosophy Considered as an Index of the Character of Any Age or Nation." The essay of 1839–40 is number iii, the Greek title of which is translated by *Checklist* as "People differ greatly about whether foreign trade is beneficial or harmful to well governed cities." (See *SPW*, pp. 205–207, for the entire latter essay.)

His study of political economy became even more intense after he took his degree, and his notebook for 1841, filled with terms, definitions, and names, reflects the immense amount of reading he did on the subject. There are some sixteen pages devoted to various charts, references, and notations concerning various theories of production, distribution, consumption, and accumulation. Clough lists definitions of such terms as "disengaged capital," "value exchangeable," "fluctuation," "rent," "luxury stimulus," "determinators," "interest," "wages," and "market"; and he mentions specifically Mill, M'Culloch, *Sartor Resartus*, Coleridge, Arnold, and Eugene Buret. This deep interest is also reflected in his personal correspondence and in a series of letters that he wrote to the editor of *The Balance*, letters which contain many ideas he later incorporated into his Retrenchment article.[6] He wrote to Gell in the summer of 1844 that he was inclined to "set to work at Political Economy, for the benefit of the rising generation." He wanted to see "if I cannot prove 'the Apostle of Anti-laissez-faire.' " (*Corr.*, I, 130 ; *PPR*, I, 92) A month before this he had written to Burbidge a rather detailed letter, part of which has already been quoted, on this subject:

> I have just received your letter with a rejoinder to my anti-non-interference philippic; . . . of course I do not mean that if [a] labourer has at present his proper proportion for 12 hours' work he should have the same sum

6. The various terms, definitions, names are found in MSS, "Oxford Notebooks, 1841." The letters to *The Balance* are as follows: "To the Editor of 'The Balance,' " *The Balance,* Jan. 23, 1846, p. 26; "Political Economy," *The Balance,* Jan. 30, 1846, p. 34; "Expensive Living," *The Balance,* Feb. 13, 1846, p. 50; "A Few Practical Hints," *The Balance,* March 6, 1846, p. 77; and "The Spirit of Trade," *The Balance,* March 20, 1846, pp. 93–94. (See *Checklist,* p. 382, and *SPW,* pp. 208–225.)

for 10: but I do believe that he has not his proper proportion, that capital tyrannizes over labour, and that
government is bound to interfere to prevent such bullying; and I do believe too that in the some way [sic] or
other the problem now solved by universal competition
or the devil take the hindmost may receive a more satisfactory solution. It is manifestly absurd that to allow
me to get my stockings ½d a pair cheaper, the operative
stocking weaver should be forced to go barefoot. It is
surely not wholly Utopian to look for some system which
will apportion the due reward to the various sets of
workmen and evade this perpetual struggle for securing
(each man to the exclusion of his neighbour) the whole
market.

(Corr., I, 126–127 ; PPR, I, 91)

His letters to *The Balance* stress even more this particular aspect of the problem, the need for some feeling of
cooperation between worker and employer and among
workers themselves. In his second letter (January 30,
1846) he attacked the selfish individualism that forms the
basis of laissez-faire:

True it is, indeed, that the results of political economy,
the pure laws of economical science, have been applied
rather to the object of expediting the low practical question, "How shall we make money," than satisfying the
high practical imperative, "Do justice to your neighbour." It has been supposed that the first of itself involved the second: the more money the country makes,
the more there will be for everyone; the larger our capital, the more labourers we shall want to work with it;
the greater the demand for labour, the greater the price
it will receive. So, again, the more thorough-going the
operation of competition, the more sure will be the re-

wards of industry, and the penalties of idleness. This
theory to many minds appears somewhat suspicious.

(See *SPW*, p. 212)

In his first letter he had emphasized the great need for a
moral view of political economy, and he repeated this idea
in his last letter of March 20: "A fundamental misconception pervading our mercantile practice, and entering perhaps into its theory, lies," he wrote, "in the belief that the
common rules of trade do in themselves constitute the laws
of fairness and honesty. A slight degree of thought would
suffice, I think, to show that, on the contrary, these rules
require the continual interference of higher principles, as
of equity; that the whole system is a mere expedient, the
best, indeed, we can lay our hands on; it serves in nine
cases, but in the tenth it fails. . . . If a plan were
brought forward to-morrow which could be warranted
more exactly and unerringly just in the rewarding of
labour, it would, I believe, be the duty and interest of the
nation, in spite of its being less productive, to adopt it."
He then concluded on a Carlylean note, condemning the
"cash-nexus" view of human relations and stressing the
need for greater social and ethical concern:

> I am not to regard myself as engaged in a petty warfare
> with all those for whom I work or who work for me. It
> is not a scramble who shall get most, and do least. We
> are not adventurers, soldiers of fortune, each man for
> himself, and chance for us all; we are servants to each
> other, soldiers in a standing army, public functionaries
> with public duties and public pay. True it is, at first
> sight it seems otherwise: as in ancient warfare, so now
> in modern trade, each man is ordered to fight for him-
> self. But the army is not therefore disbanded; we are still

under orders. And as in modern warfare it has been found that organised co-operation is, if less stimulant of individual energy, nevertheless more effective of general success, so may it be in future days with modern trade. But in this way, or in that, whatever the tactics, whatever the commands, we are still to all intents fellow-soldiers, a single army engaged for the common good against a single enemy, the earth, which we have to "subdue," the elements, whose resources we must force.

(See SPW, pp. 223, 224, 225)

With the passing years Clough's objections to laissez-faire became more specific than the general one of man's inhumanity to man. In addition to the broad charges against the system—the tyranny of capital and the lack of "due reward" for the worker—Clough came to condemn the system for bringing about (1) the absence of joy in work, which, in turn, resulted in the poor quality of the products being made, and (2) the general lack of good taste in the age for which it was responsible. These points are cited by other Victorians—Huxley, Arnold, Ruskin, Morris—but the actual language and general development of Clough's argument suggest the dominant influence of Carlyle, whose "sociological realism" appealed greatly to Clough.[7]

Clough's specific points are listed clearly and precisely in his review of Norton's *Recent Social Theories*. "The crying evil . . . of the present system of unrestricted competition," Clough writes, "is not so much the distress of the workmen as the extreme slovenliness and badness of their work. The joy and satisfaction of making really good

7. Jerome H. Buckley, *The Victorian Temper*, Cambridge, Mass., 1951, p. 37.

things is destroyed by the criminal eagerness to make them
to suit the market. The love of art, which, quite as much
as virtue, is its own reward, used in the old times to penetrate down as far as to the meanest manufacture of kettles,
for example, and pots. With us, on the contrary, the
miserable truckling to the bad taste of the multitude has
gradually stolen up into the very regions of the highest
art—into architecture, sculpture, painting, music, literature. Nay, has it not infected even morality and religion?"
(*SPW*, p. 267; *PPR*, I, 416) Clough's main ideas in this
passage appear in Carlyle's various works. His concern
with lack of good taste, for instance, is a direct echo of
Carlyle's distinction in *Signs of the Times* (1829) between "mechanical" and "dynamical" ages and his desig-
nation of his own as mechanical. "Let us observe," Carlyle writes, "how the mechanical genius of our time has
diffused itself into quite other provinces. Not the external
and physical alone is managed by machinery, but the in-
ternal and spiritual also." (*Works*, XV, 466) In the same
manner we find Clough's other concern, the lack of satisfaction to be found in work, stressed by Carlyle in *Past
and Present*. "It is not to die, or even to die of hunger," he
states, "that makes a man wretched; many men have died;
all men must die. . . . But it is to live miserable we know
not why; to work sore and yet gain nothing." (*Works*,
XIX, 203–204)

Clough's insistence on "connecting" with others in this
world rather than worrying about what the next might be
is evident not only in his comments on laissez-faire; it is
also the basis for his ideas on property and classes, areas
which reflect his liberal thought as well as his social awareness. Clough owes a great deal to Carlyle in his attitude

towards property, for the latter's views were less conservative than Dr. Arnold's (whose ideas also had some effect on
Clough's thoughts) and thus were more compatible to
Clough's own solutions to social and economic problems.
Arnold, for instance, insists that an individual has the
right to control his own land and that justice requires the
observance of laws governing the rights of ownership;
both Carlyle and Clough, however, insist on equity above
justice. They both regard the possession of land as a privilege that places a heavy responsibility upon the possessor.
"Who," asks Carlyle, "made the Land of England? . . .
'We!' answer the much-*consuming* Aristocracy. . . . 'It
is we that made it; or are the heirs . . . of those who did.' "
But Carlyle retorts that the land belongs to "the Almighty
Maker and to all His Children of Men that have worked
well on it." In typical Carlylean fashion he tells these
misguided aristocrats: "I say you did *not* make the land of
England; and by the possession of it, you *are* bound to
furnish guidance and governance to England. That is the
law of your position on this God's-Earth. . . . My lords
and gentlemen, it were better for you to arise and begin
doing your work, than sit there and plead parchments!"
(*Past and Present, Works,* XIX, 170, 171, 173)

Clough agrees with Carlyle, making the fullest statement on this subject in his Retrenchment article. The
failure of the potato crop in Ireland had caused great distress, and Clough was deeply moved by the apparent un-
concern of many people in England, especially those whom
Carlyle called the "unworking aristocracy." These people,
Clough warns, must remember their responsibilities: "The
Institution of Property . . . is all well enough as a human expedient to secure its reward to industry, and pro-

tect the provident labourer against the careless and idle.
But for half-million-per-annum fortunes, fifty-mile-long
estates, and may-I-not-do-what-I-please-with-my-own pro-
prietors, some other justification, it would seem, must be
sought." [8] Clough, like Carlyle, feels that the land belongs
to God and all His Children; even to those whose subsistence ultimately derives from it: "Ultimately," he states,
"it is the earth that forms our wealth and our subsistence.
Philosophers and merchants, poets and shopkeepers, soldiers, sailors, tinkers, tailors—in our most spiritual, as in
our most material productions, we all alike start in this, in
the earth have . . . our work to work at. And 'the earth
hath He given to the children of men.' " The owners have
not rights, but responsibilities. "The property is not your
own: scarcely your own at any time; during times of
calamity in no wise, except to do good with and distribute." And he concludes with an admonition that recalls
Carlyle's injunction against "pleading parchments": "O
ye, born to be rich, . . . let me advise you to hesitate ere
you venture the question, May I not do what I like with
my own? ere you meddle with such edge-tools as the subject of property. Some one, I fear, might be found to look
up your title-deeds, and to quote inconvenient Scriptures." (*SPW*, pp. 232, 237, 231–232; *PPR*, I, 280–281;
286; 280)

These views on property foreshadow Clough's opinions
on the related topic of class structure, and again his ideas
are similar to those of Dr. Arnold and Carlyle. All three
men sympathize with the working class; yet all three see

8. *SPW*, p. 232; *PPR*, I, 280; see also Clough's condemnation of ex-
travagance in "Expensive Living," *The Balance*, Feb. 13, 1846, p. 50;
SPW, 217–221.

the need for the existence of various classes, including the aristocracy. Both Carlyle and Clough would agree with Arnold that equality is "a dream of a madman, or the passion of a fiend." [9] But while Arnold, again the most conservative, is more intent on pointing out the wide gap between classes than with placing the blame on one or the other for the gap, Carlyle and Clough are more outspoken about designating the responsibility. Both are "anti-aristocratic," pointing to the "sublime indifference" of the rich as the reason for the separation of the high and low classes. Carlyle's ideas are pungently stated in his chapters on the "Gospel of Dilettantism" and "Unworking Aristocracy" in *Past and Present;* Clough's are found in his Retrenchment article, his letters from France during his stay there in 1848, and in the *Bothie,* written shortly after his resignation.

His letters from France are particularly revealing. After his resignation from Oxford, Clough had gone directly to Paris, which was then in the midst of a revolution. He arrived on May 1, 1848; in February of that year, after three days of rioting and bloodshed, Louis Philippe had been forced to abdicate and a republic had been proclaimed. Clough, of course, wholeheartedly supported it, telling Tom Arnold that "next to myself," Palgrave is accounted "the wildest and most écervelé republican going. I myself apropos of a letter of Matt's which he directed to Citizen Clough, Oriel Lyceum, Oxford, bear that title par excellence." (*Corr.,* I, 216; *PPR,* I, 133) His anti-aristocratic sentiment was strengthened as he watched the

9. Thomas Arnold, *Miscellaneous Works,* London, 1845, p. 182. This volume contains extracts from Arnold's own paper, *The Englishman's Register,* and his letters to *The Sheffield Courant* and *The Hertford Reformer.*

progress of the revolution. "I growl occasionally," he wrote
to Stanley, "at the sight of aristocratic equipages which
begin to peep out again, and trust that the National Assembly will in its wisdom forbid the use of livery servants."
(*Corr.*, I, 206–207; *PPR*, I, 123) He was not, however,
lulled into false optimism about the permanent results of
the event he was witnessing. On May 14 he wrote to his sister that he did not expect much good to come of the present
Assembly: "It is extremely shopkeeperish and merchantish
in its feelings, and won't set to work at the organization of
labour at all, at all. But will prefer going to war to keep
the people amused, rather than open any disagreeable
social questions." (*Corr.*, I, 204; *PPR*, I, 120) Clough's
prophecy came true. The following day the working
classes, believing that the government had broken its promise to provide employment, staged a riot. The mob succeeded in turning out the Assembly, but the National
Guard quelled the riot. Clough, in his best Carlylean
strain, expressed his disappointment to Stanley: "Ichabod, Ichabod, the glory is departed. Liberty, Equality,
and Fraternity driven back by shopkeeping bayonet, hides
her red cap in dingiest St. Antoine. . . . Meantime the
glory and the freshness of the dream is departed. . . .
Wherefore—Bring forth, ye millionaires, the three-month-
hidden carriages; rub clean, ye new nobles, the dusty em-
blazonries; . . . the world begins once more to move on
its axis and draw on its kid gloves." (*Corr.*, I, 207; *PPR*,
I, 123–124)

Clough's *Bothie* also contains these anti-aristocratic
sentiments, most of which are uttered by Elspie Mackaye,
the heroine, and Philip, the hero, a radical, whom Clough
introduces as

> *Hewson a radical hot, hating lords and scorning ladies,*
> *Silent mostly, but often reviling in fire and fury*
> *Feudal tenures, mercantile lords, competition and*
> *   bishops,*
> *Liveries, armorial bearings, amongst other matters the*
> *   Game-laws.*
>
> (*Poems*, p. 120)

Philip's various speeches contain many of Clough's opinions. To his fellow-Oxonians, for instance, who are speaking of "noble ladies," Philip replies:

> *Sick of the very names of your Lady Augustas and*
> *   Floras*
> *Am I, as ever I was of the dreary botanical titles*
> *Of the exotic plants, their antitypes, in the hot-house.*
>
> (*Poems*, p. 122)

Elspie later seconds him when, after they are engaged, she tells Philip:

> *I will not be a lady,*
>
>   *   *   *
>
> *I could not bear to sit and be waited upon by footmen,*
> *No, not even by women.*
>
> (*Poems*, p. 167)

She gets her wish, for she and Philip, after he earns his degree, are married and go off to New Zealand to begin life as co-workers, to hew, and dig, and subdue the earth. They find in the Antipodes the duty that they were meant to do; they both achieve the true dignity that comes to those who are content to do their duty.

It is natural that Clough's "anti-aristocratic" view
would lead him to stress two other related topics, politics
and liberty. This same sentiment, for instance, plays a
prominent part in his attitude towards domestic and international affairs. In domestic affairs he seems at first to
have a cynical attitude, but this cynicism is of the same
kind that appears in his satiric poetry: that which serves
as a cover for his real emotions of disappointment and distrust, in this case, the disappointment in and the distrust
of both the Liberal and Conservative parties. He felt that
both parties were not at all interested in the problems vital
to the people who really needed help in England; both
were opportunistic, over-concerned with trade and mercantile problems, not enough concerned with the problems
of the lower classes. The obvious failure of parliament to
support any reforms dealing with the working classes and
the sympathetic attitude of both parties to "laissez-faire
and devil take the hindmost" led him to make sarcastic
comments and to be sympathetic to the aims of Bright and
the Radical party in their efforts to secure reforms.
"Bright's agitation will bear fruits," Clough wrote to Norton in January, 1859. "Bright is scoffed at in the Metro-
politan papers and at all Clubs—but his hold on the country is such as no MP whatever except himself, possesses—
and in the main the course he has taken is right, I think."
(*Corr.*, II, 562; *PPR*, I, 238)

The lack of any real difference between the parties disturbed Clough, for since there was no real choice, people
were becoming more and more apathetic: "There is as yet
but a very light ripple on the face of our political waters,"
he told Norton. "The interest taken in these matters by

the nations [sic] seems to grow less and less. People will not mind if the other party come in,—but they don't want Palmerston again." (*Corr.*, II, 557; *PPR*, I, 237) To Clough both parties were "aristocratic," kept apart only by personal jealousies; if necessary they would not hesitate to unite against a common "unaristocratic" opponent. Reporting to Norton in July, 1860, he wrote that there was talk of "a grand fusion of the Conservative and Liberal-Conservative parties, modern Tories and modern Whigs making one solid national defence against Bright and the Radicals," but that he could not conceive of such a unity "unless Bright and the Radicals become formidable indeed." His own conclusion was that the future was "quite obscure." (*PPR*, I, 244)

Clough's sympathy for the views of Bright and the Radical party did not lead him to trust naively in the "people"; he by no means believed that giving the "people" the power to vote would cure England's ills. On the contrary, he had no desire to disrupt the present political and social hierarchy; like Carlyle, he wanted the aristocracy to assume its responsibility. His practical objections to the placing of too much trust in the "people" appear in his review of Norton's *Recent Social Theories*. "A people," he writes, "can be the slave of cupidity and resentment; a people can be pusillanimous, dastardly, and base; a people can be also fiendishly inhuman; the fears and passions of a people, when once excited, are more hopelessly irrational, more wildly uncontrollable, more extensively ruinous, more apallingly terrible, than those of councils and kings. . . . A people . . . we conceive, however generous and well-meaning, is apt to be a little too rough-handed to deal properly with nice points of fairness and

honour, and delicate questions of feeling." [10] His ability to
distinguish between liberalism and radicalism and his refusal to be drawn into the position of advocating change
simply for the sake of change itself had been gained in
France where, in 1848, he had seen what could happen to
idealistic theories when they were subjected to the harsh
exigencies of practical day-to-day politics.

His desire for the "triumph of genuine liberty" was as
pervasive in his views on international politics as it was in
his views on domestic affairs; and the disappointment his
"liberal" hopes received in England was paralleled by his
experiences with foreign affairs. He found no realization
of his political ideals in events abroad or in the part his
own country played in them. His letters and *Amours de
Voyage* reveal particularly his sympathy with the Italian
people in their efforts to become independent, his hatred
of the Pope and of France, especially Louis Napoleon,
who, he felt, had betrayed the Italians, and his disgust
with England, which had refused to help those fighting for
independence. His sorrow over the lack of success of the
Italian revolutionists in Rome in 1849 was as deeply felt
as that which he had experienced in the failure of his own
parliament to grant any reforms to the working classes
of England.

Clough's sympathy for the Italian people was grounded
in personal observation, for he was a witness to their
struggles. He visited Rome in April, 1849. In February of

10. *SPW*, pp. 259–260; *PPR*, I, 412. See also his student essay *"Vox
Populi Vox Dei,"* Nov. 20, 1840, in MSS, "English Essays, 1837–1841."
(*SPW*, p. 348; *Checklist*, p. 381) See also *Checklist*, pp. 388–389 (nos. 46,
47, 48) for more references to his ideas on equality and, in particular, his
opposition to the Carlylean doctrine of might. Number 47, "Might versus
Right in Economics and Politics," and number 48, "British and American
Imperialism," are printed in *SPW*, pp. 249–257.

that year Pope Pius IX, failing to effect a compromise with the revolutionists, had fled the city in disguise, and a Republic had been established under the triumvirate of Mazzini, Armellini, and Saffi. The French, wishing to prevent intervention by Austria and determined to restore the Pope, attacked the city on April 30 with troops under General Oudinot. Led by Garibaldi, the Italians successfully repelled the initial attack of the French forces, which then settled down to besiege the city. A short time later they received reinforcements and on June 30 successfully attacked and defeated the Italian troops. On July 3 a new constitution restoring the power of the Pope was proclaimed, and the ill-fated Roman Republic was no more. Clough wrote *Amours de Voyage* while he was living in the besieged city, and he used the fighting as the background for the story which tells of the frustrated and frustrating love affair between a sensitive young Englishman, Claude, and a daughter of a nouveau-riche family, the Trevellyns. The *Amours* will be discussed at length later; at this point its importance lies in the observations by its author on the political scene.

While he is not to be regarded as Clough himself, Claude is constantly making comments which reflect Clough's hatred of the French and his admiration of the Italians in their fight for political independence. We find Claude writing (Clough employs the epistolary method) to his friend Eustace, for instance:

I, nevertheless, let me say it,
Could in my soul of souls, this day, with the Gaul at the gates, shed
One true tear for thee, thou poor little Roman Republic!

What, with the German restored, with Sicily safe to the
  Bourbon,
Not leave one poor corner for native Italian exertion?
France, it is foully done!

(*Poems*, p. 187)

He also indicates his disgust with England's inaction, as
Claude sarcastically comments:

         . . . you, poor foolish England,—
You, who a twelvemonth ago said nations must choose
  for themselves, you
Could not, of course, interfere.

(*Poems*, p. 187)

Clough's admiration for the heroic Italian fighters and
their leader Mazzini is apparent as Claude tells Eustace:

Ah, 'tis an excellent race,—and even in old degradation,
Under a rule that enforces to flattery, lying, and cheat-
  ing,
E'en under Pope and Priest, a nice and natural people.
Oh, could they but be allowed this chance of redemption!
  —but clearly
That is not likely to be. Meantime, notwithstanding all
  journals,
Honour for once to the tongue and the pen of the elo-
  quent writer!
Honour to speech! and all honour to thee, thou noble
  Mazzini!

(*Poems*, pp. 194–195)

Clough himself rightly insisted that it was a mistake to
regard the hero and the writer as one and the same; but
the same praise for the Italians and Mazzini and the senti-

ments against France uttered by Claude are present in Clough's letters. He wrote at length to Palgrave in April to describe an interview he had with Mazzini, and the following month he told Tom Arnold how much he admired Mazzini and his countrymen: "You will have heard of our driving back the French and amongst many lies would probably detect the fact that the French never entered the town, but were killed and wounded and taken by shot from the walls and by sorties. . . . Whether the Roman Republic will stand I don't know, but it has shown under Mazzini's inspiration a wonderful energy, and a glorious generosity: and at any rate has shaken to its foundation the Odillon-Barrot ministry, which I trust may yet go to its own place." (*Corr.*, I, 255; *PPR*, I, 147) His letters during June, July, and August, when the city was under siege, are full of references to various French and Italian maneuvers, but always there is the anti-French, pro-Italian sentiment. And at the end there was disappointment and frustration. "This, my dear Tom," he wrote to Tom Arnold in June, "is being written while guns are going off—there—there—there. For these blackguard French are attacking us again. May the Lord scatter and confound them." (*Corr.*, I, 256; *PPR*, I, 150) To his friend Shairp he complained in the same vein: "No; your letter won't go to-day: for the French are attacking us— there! there! 'But do Thou unto them as unto the Midianites. O my God, make them like unto a wheel.'" (*PPR*, I, 151) In spite of his exhortations, the French were victorious, and Clough could only exclaim to Tom Arnold, "Unto this has come our grand Lib[erty], Eq[uality] and Frat [ernity] revolution!" (*Corr.*, I, 256; *PPR*, I, 151) and to Palgrave in an even more depressed tone: "I am full of

admiration of Mazzini. But, on the whole, 'Farewell,
politics, utterly!'" (*PPR*, I, 164)

But Clough was far too keenly alert to events going on
in the world ever to bid farewell to politics; and ten years
after the downfall of the Roman Republic of 1849, he
was again taking an avid interest in the attempts of the
Italians to free themselves from the tyranny of Austria.
The same burning desire for freedom that had led to the
scattered revolutions throughout Italy in 1848–49 was responsible for the fresh attempts the Italians made in 1859.
Through the skillful political maneuvering of Napoleon
III, France joined Piedmont in a war against Austria to
drive the latter out of Italy. In two months of fighting,
May and June, the allies forced the Austrian troops to
retreat, taking Milan and driving the Austrians into
Venetia. There seemed to be no doubt that at last the Austrians would be driven out of Italy, but Napoleon III now
began to realize the possible repercussions of this action.
First, many people in France, especially the clerics, were
opposed to the Emperor's Italian policy. Second, Napoleon
had not foreseen the enthusiastic response of all the other
Italians to the withdrawal of the Austrian forces; in
northern Italy, as the Austrians left, Tuscany, Parma,
Modena, and the Papal States asked permission to join
Piedmont, a turn of events not to Napoleon's liking. While
he had no objection to Piedmont's being free from Austrian rule, he had no desire to see a completely unified and
powerful Italy immediately next to France. Third, the
English and Prussians were threatening to interfere in
behalf of Austria, fearing, perhaps, that France was becoming too powerfully entrenched in Italy. Consequently,
Napoleon concluded a peace treaty with Austria—se-

cretly, without the knowledge of Cavour and the Italians —on July 8, under the terms of which Lombardy was ceded to Piedmont, Venetia remained with the Hapsburgs, and central Italy was restored to the Pope and the deposed princes. Cavour and the Italian people were keenly disappointed by this duplicity and political maneuvering, and so was Clough, who saw in the person of Napoleon III the epitome of all that was inimical to the establishment of "genuine liberty." During this period, as he had ten years before, he displayed an intense hatred of tyranny— in this case in the persons of the Pope and Napoleon III— and a sincere admiration of those fighting for their liberty, particularly patriots like Garibaldi and Mazzini.

He constantly questioned Napoleon's sincerity in wanting to liberate the Italians, especially in the light of his dealings with the Pope. He wrote to Norton, for instance: "We who live nearer to Louis Napoleon, with only the Channel, and not the whole Atlantic to divide and protect us from him, do not feel quite the same liberty to indulge the natural feelings of enthusiasm in witnessing his aggrandisement in Europe, though it be merely as a liberator that he effects it at present." And then Clough let his anti-Papal feelings get the best of him. "One thing I devoutly hope; that, with French influence predominating in Italy, the Pope will go to the dogs, with all his canaille accompanying." (*PPR*, I, 240)

After Napoleon had made his secret treaty with the Austrians, Clough was especially distrustful and bitter; he wrote to Norton: "Here meantime we are reading the last bulletins of that wonderful melodramatic genius— Napoleon II [sic]—of which what can be said—L'Em-

pire, c'est la Paix!—Certainly one did not desire the en-
franchisement of Italy to be effected by his means—and
one may hope also that the general result will be to dam-
age him and his dynasty." (*Corr.*, II, 569; *PPR*, I, 240)
Clough never did lose his suspicion of Napoleon, and as late
as October, 1860, he revealed his fear of the French emperor's designs on Italy: "Lord John Russell they say has
been exciting anger in the French imperial circles by talking, when on the Queen's German tour, against L[ouis]
Napoleon—L. N. is said to be very cross, having offered
his company at Warsaw and had it declined. However, if he
is cross *that* way all the better. But why does he keep his
paw on the patrimony of St. Peter and exclude the lawful
heir Victor Emanuel?—" (*Corr.*, II, 581; *PPR*, I, 246) It
was a little over a year later that Clough died in Florence,
and to the very end he retained this active interest in politics. Napoleon III was to him a living figure not to be
trusted, and also a symbol of tyranny and oppression,
against which Clough fought all his life.

Perhaps the best illustration of how closely knit were
Clough's social, political, and economic ideas with his religious ones is his concept of liberty; for in seeking to define the term he attempted to reconcile the opposing ideas
of man's freedom—political, religious, social, economic—
with man's idea of responsibility towards himself, his fellow men, and God. It is at this point that duty and service
become important; if one is able to realize their significance, he is able to solve the dilemma of connecting religion and daily life in all its social, political, and economic
complexities.

One of the fruitful ways to see Clough's distinctive solution to this problem is to compare it with Carlyle's. Both men indicate their disagreement with what they regard the current definition of liberty in an industrial and democratic society: "each man for himself." "Liberty," says Carlyle in *Past and Present*, "I am told is a divine thing. Liberty when it becomes the 'Liberty to die by starvation' is not so divine!" (*Works*, XIX, 205–206) Clough also rejects the notion that liberty is simply unrestricted freedom: "The mature free will of the grown man looks back . . . with no little scorn, upon the bygone puerile spontaneities of the time when he did as he liked. There are periods . . . when expansion is the first of necessities. . . . But because we would be rid of existing restrictions, it does not follow that restriction of all kinds is an evil." (*SPW*, p. 264; *PPR*, I, 414–415) Both then go on to provide new definitions of liberty; for them, liberty consists of the individual's finding the work that he is best fitted to do, thus becoming an integral part of the society in which he lives. "The true liberty of a man," Carlyle insists, ". . . consisted in his finding out, or being forced to find out the right path, and to walk thereon. To learn, or to be taught, what work he actually was able for; and then by permission, persuasion, and even compulsion, to set about doing of the same! That is his true blessedness, honour, 'liberty' and maximum of wellbeing." (*Past and Present, Works*, XIX, 205) Clough too looks upon liberty as finding one's true relationship to one's fellow man through his work. "The true comfort to the soldiers, serving in the great industrial army of arts, commerce, and manufactures, is . . . to show them that what they are now doing is good and useful service to the community; to call upon them to do it well and thoroughly; and to teach them how they may;—and all this quite irrespectively of any prospects, either of making a fortune or living on into a good time." (*SPW*, pp. 267–268; *PPR*, I, 416–417)

The similarities and the differences are apparent in these last two quotations. Both men see duty as a means to establish man's relationship to his fellow men. But Carlyle seems to insist that this work be work, no matter what kind; his stress is on the work *per se*. In *Sartor Resartus* he had said: "But indeed Conviction, were it never so excellent, is worthless till it convert itself into Conduct. . . . '*Do the Duty which lies nearest thee*,' which thou knowest to be a Duty. Thy second Duty will already have become clearer." (*Works*, XIV, 148) Clough at times echoes this sentiment, especially in his poem "*Qui Laborat, Orat*"; but, ever mindful of the need for "good and useful service to the community," he shifts Carlyle's emphasis and gives it a distinctly Christian interpretation. Rather than putting the stress on work *per se*, Clough puts the emphasis on work that is of benefit to others. By serving one's fellow man to the best of his ability, one is ultimately serving God. All that has been said about his concept of duty in the discussion of his religious thought—his stress on the doing rather than the waiting, on the necessity of positive action in this world, on the essential truths being found "everywhere, but above all in our own work"— would apply here to his social, political, and economic thought as well. And the same is true of his own acts in his lifetime, especially his work in the Education Office and his service for Florence Nightingale. Perhaps the best example of this attitude strictly from the social point of view is found in his review of Norton's book. "Let it not be forgotten," he cautioned, "that the object of human society

is not the mere 'culinary' one of securing equal apportionments of meat and drink to all its members. Men combine
for some higher objects; and to that higher object it is, in
their social capacity, the *privilege* and real happiness of
individuals to sacrifice themselves. The highest political
watchword is not Liberty, Equality, Fraternity, nor yet
Solidarity, but *Service*." (*SPW*, p. 267; *PPR*, I, 416)

It is impossible, then, to separate Clough's ideas on society and religion, for they all culminate in his concept of
service, of doing one's duty for one's fellow man while here
on earth. One critic has objected as being beside the point,
and rightly so, the claim that Clough did not write his
poetry, but lived it. It is not misleading, however, to say
that Clough not only did write about what he believed, but
lived his beliefs. Failure to understand Clough's aims has
resulted in failure to understand his actions and the real
success he achieved in his lifetime. His religious position,
based on his recognition of God, his belief in the essentials
of Christianity, and the concept of duty as service, was both
valid and practical for him. His social, political, and economic ideas, based on a sympathy for the oppressed, a
genuine love of liberty, and a clear recognition of the need
for service to society, were equally valid and workable.
Basic to all of these, and unrecognized up to now, is his
"positive naturalism," which enabled him to accept man
and his actions for what they are rather than what some
theory or system might say they ought to be. He was able
to see man as capable of virtuous and sinful actions. He
was also able to write about these with complete honesty
and acceptance, knowing that man was essentially good,
capable of "ordering and distributing his native goodness"
so that he could live "as befits him." His positive and nat-

ural acceptance of human nature, his refusal to shut his
eyes to fact and truth, and his essentially optimistic faith
in man's ability to assert his true dignity by means of his
service to his fellow man and thus to God are the distinctive features of his thought. If Clough's unique contribution to Victorian literature is ever to be seen, it must begin
with a clear comprehension of his thought. And full recognition of his contribution must come with the understanding and appreciation of his art, which is, after all,
the means by which he revealed and expressed most effectively and forcefully his views on man and God. Like
Matthew Arnold, Clough came to believe that poetry must
be at bottom a criticism of life; consequently, it is impossible to talk of Clough the man as separate from Clough
the artist.

ᴁ *Clough's Art*

(A) *The poetic theory*

If the problem with Clough's religious and social thought
has been one of learning to understand exactly what he
meant rather than taking for granted that since he was
not an orthodox believer he was therefore a skeptic and a
failure, the problem with his art is one of learning to take
him at his word rather than believing what critics, and
sometimes sympathetic ones, have insisted that he meant to
say or do. He has to be rescued from those who are so eager
to have his poetry read and appreciated that they make
him either into their own image or into some image that
they feel is more appealing to the modern reader. This
approach has resulted in Clough's being placed in a wide
range of poetic traditions and his poetry's being re-

garded as fiction, autobiography, Freudian or Jungian sublimations, Byronic exercises, religious hymns, or realistic, ironic commentaries on life.[1] To emphasize his "modernity," much has been made of his technique, with the result that the poetry has become at times merely a convenient focal point for a discussion of prosodic elements. Certainly, Clough was an artist, and his poetry must be discussed in terms of technical achievement and artistic skills. It also, however, needs to be placed in the context of his time and thought and discussed in the light of his own poetic theory.[2]

For Clough, as for many of his contemporaries, poetry was basically the disclosure of a man's character, the reflection of his nature, the verbal expression of his innermost being. In his lecture on the development of English

1. For these various approaches see J. M. Robertson, *New Essays towards a Critical Method*, London, 1897, pp. 301–330; Humbert Wolfe, "Arthur Hugh Clough," *The Eighteen-Sixties,* ed. John Drinkwater, Cambridge, 1932, pp. 20–50; the introduction by Michael Roberts to *The Faber Book of Modern Verse,* London, 1936; Chorley, and Houghton. For a summary of critical commentary on Clough's work, see the chapter entitled "The Critical Tradition" in Houghton, pp. 1–26.

2. Besides his letters, the following sources, found in *SPW* and *PPR,* I, contain much of the materials from which may be gathered Clough's poetic theory: "A Long Talk," *SPW,* pp. 39–57; "The Moral Effect of Works of Satire," *SPW,* pp. 63–65; "Dryden and His Times," (*SPW,* pp. 85–122; *PPR,* I, 327–334, entitled "On the Formation of Classical English"); "Poetry and Skepticism," *SPW,* p. 123; "The Development of English Literature," (*SPW,* pp. 124–142; *PPR,* I, 335–356, entitled "Lecture on the Development of English Literature from Chaucer to Wordsworth"); "Lecture on Wordsworth," (*SPW,* pp. 107–122; *PPR,* I, 307–326, entitled "Lecture on the Poetry of Wordsworth"); "Recent English Poetry," (*SPW,* pp. 143–171; *PPR,* I, 357–384, entitled "Review of Some Poems by Alexander Smith and Matthew Arnold"); "Letters of Parepidemus, I and II," (*SPW,* pp. 172–186; *PPR,* I, 385–402, entitled "Two Letters of Parepidemus"). Other important sources are, of course, "Memoir" in *PPR,* I, 1–54; MSS, "English Essays, 1837–1841"; "Oxford Notebooks, 1841"; and *RM.* The remarks by Houghton in *Checklist* and by Trawick in *SPW* regarding the various bibliographical and textual developments of these essays are most valuable and should be consulted.

literature he states that the works of Shakespeare and Milton reflect their characters. Shakespeare wrote the plays that he did because he was characteristically of a "balanced speculative" nature. Milton, on the other hand, wrote the poetry that he did because he was "strongly, deliberately, seriously, irreversibly committed; walking as in sight of God, as in the profound almost rigid conviction, that this one, and no other of all those many paths is or can be, for the just and upright spirit possible—self-predestined as it were, . . . to a single moral and religious aim." (*SPW*, p. 128; *PPR*, I, 341, 342)

But Clough's concept of the nature of poetry is complicated by the moral and ethical basis of his poetic theory. The end of poetry for Clough is primarily moral; therefore, since poetry is the reflection of a man's essential nature, the value of the poetry becomes dependent on the character of the poet, and it becomes necessary to examine the poet's "character and his view of life" to see if he has sincerely and accurately expressed this character and this view in his poetry. If the poet is of a virtuous nature, the more accurately he is able to reflect this "virtue" in his poetry, the better his poetry will be. This belief is behind Clough's implication that Wordsworth is a great poet because he "succeeded beyond the other poets of the time . . . in making his verse permanently true to his genius and his moral frame." (*SPW*, p. 117; *PPR*, I, 320)

It is important, however, to see that Clough's concept of the moral or virtuous man is not simply the view of an outwardly pious or religious individual; it is much closer to Carlyle's view of the "moral" individual, the man virtuously related to the universe: "To know a thing," Carlyle wrote in *Heroes and Hero-Worship*, "what we can call knowing, a man must first love the thing, sympathize with it; that is, be *virtuously* related to it. If he have not the justice to put down his own selfishness at every turn, . . . how shall he know?" [3] Clough echoes Carlyle's words as, after condemning Byron's "hot career of wilfulness" and Scott's "easy existence," he praises Wordsworth's "dignified, elevated, serious, significant, and truly human . . . homely and frugal life in the cottage at Grasmere." (*SPW*, p. 118; *PPR*, I, 321) The emphasis remains here, as elsewhere, on the acceptance of and sympathy for the "truly human" rather than the pretentiously artificial.

Clough's view of the poet and the nature of poetry is most clearly brought out in his lecture on the poetry of Wordsworth, for it is principally because of this approach that he prefers Wordsworth to almost any other poet. Clough inquires into "the worth of that genius and moral frame[,] the amount of the real significance of his character and view of life," and he finds that while Byron exhibits an "ebullient overflowing life, refusing all existing restrictions," and while Scott exhibits a "free vigorous animal nature ready to accept whatever things Earth has to offer," Wordsworth's pre-eminence consists in having "attained a law," and in exercising "a lordship by right divine over passions and desires." The similarity of this statement to Carlyle's admiration for the man who

3. *Heroes and Hero-Worship, Works,* XIV, 334. It is difficult, in the light of Clough's ideas in this respect, to see how Houghton comes to the conclusion that Byron is one of Clough's "heroes" (p. 82) or how he arrives at the idea (p. 228) that Clough preferred the later Byron from the remarks in *SPW,* pp. 114, 117; *PPR,* I, 317, 320. In these pages Clough is contrasting Wordsworth's "elevation and fixity" to Byron's willful behavior, and his conjecture as to what Byron might have been if he had survived Missolonghi can hardly be taken for a preference for the later Byron. See also his praise of Wordsworth in "A Long Talk," *RM,* I, 311–319; *SPW ,* pp. 39–47.

has the justice to "put down his own selfishness at every turn" is obvious.

His admiration for the character of Wordsworth becomes transferred to the poetry of Wordsworth. Wordsworth is a greater artist than either Byron or Scott precisely because his poetry more perfectly expresses his essentially moral nature. "His poems," writes Clough, "do more perfectly and exquisitely and unintermittedly express his real meaning and significance and character than do the poems of either Scott or Byron." Contrasting Wordsworth with the two "lesser" writers, Clough cites what for him is indisputable proof of Wordsworth's superiority. Wordsworth did not "sweep" or "carry" away with him the "exulting hearts of youth," as did Byron; he did not "win the eager and attentive ear of high and low, at home and abroad in the entertainment of immortal Waverley novels"; but he did "lay slowly the ponderous foundations of pillars to sustain man's moral fabric"; he did "fix a centre around which the chaotic elements of human impulse and desire might take solid form and move in their ordered ellipses"; he did "originate a spiritual stability." And all this, to Clough, was "greater than sweeping over glad blue waters or inditing immortal novels." (*SPW*, pp. 117, 113, 118–119; *PPR*, I, 320, 316, 322)

The belief that the poet must be "moral" and that poetry is the reflection of his virtuous nature directly affects Clough's thinking on the two closely related questions of subject matter and function. Clough felt that poetry should deal with what he called the "obvious facts of human nature"; that is, with subjects that have some significance to all men, rather than with pastoral scenes or

with stories from the classical past that might be of some
interest to only a select few. Alexander Smith is praised
for writing about and using images from the present,
while Arnold and even Wordsworth are condemned for
making too much of classical myths and of nature. "Is it
not . . . an easy matter," asks Clough, "to sit under a
green tree by a purling brook, and indite pleasing stanzas
on the beauties of Nature and fresh air?" Or, he asks, is it
"so very great an exploit to wander out into the pleasant
fields of Greek or Latin mythology, and reproduce, with
more or less of modern adaptation,—'the shadows/ Faded
and pale, yet immortal, of Faunus, the Nymphs, and the
Graces?'" Should not poetry, he says, to gain the ear of
the multitudes, to shake the hearts of men, "deal more
than at present it usually does, with general wants, ordinary feelings, the obvious rather than the rare facts of
human nature?" (*SPW*, p. 144; *PPR*, I, 360–361)
Smith's *A Life-Drama* has the advantage of not being
"mere pastoral sweet piping from the country," and the
images of the poem are praised because they are drawn
from "the busy seats of industry" and are "lifelike, immediate and firsthand." And Arnold's *Tristram and Iseult* is
better than his *Empedocles on Etna* because Clough prefers the "human passions and sorrows of the Knight and
the Queen" to the "high, and . . . pseudo-Greek inflation
of the philosopher musing above the crater, and the boy
Callicles, singing myths upon the mountains." (*SPW*,
pp. 145–146, 159; *PPR*, I, 362, 373) Both Arnold and
Wordsworth, according to Clough, are inclined to put too
much stress on nature. In the former he notes a disposition
to "assign too high a place to what is called Nature"; the

latter, instead of using the phenomena of external nature as analogies of what is truly great—human nature—is guilty of regarding these phenomena as being the truly great, all important, and pre-eminently wonderful things of the universe. "The Poet of Nature he may perhaps be," concludes Clough, somewhat sharply, "but this sort of writing does justice to the proper worth [and] dignity neither of Man *nor* Nature." (*SPW*, p. 121; *PPR*, I, 325)

To Clough the greatness of poetry lies in its application to life. Specifically, poetry has two principal aims. First, it should teach the significance of and give some purpose to our own petty lives and works. Second, it should indicate to us our relationship to the "purer existence." Could not poetry, he asks:

> attempt to convert into beauty and thankfulness, or at least into some form and shape, some feeling, at any rate, of content—the actual, palpable things with which our every-day life is concerned; introduce into business and weary task-work a character and a soul of purpose and reality; intimate to us relations which, in our unchosen, peremptorily-appointed posts, in our grievously narrow and limited spheres of action, we still, in and through all, retain to some central, celestial fact? Could it not console us with a sense of significance, if not of dignity, in that often dirty, or at least dingy, work which it is the lot of so many of us to have to do, and which some one or other, after all, must do? Might it not divinely condescend to all infirmities; . . . exclude nothing, least of all guilt and distress . . . ; not content itself merely with talking of what may be better elsewhere, but seek also to deal with what *is* here? . . . Cannot the Divine Song in some way indicate to us our unity, . . . with those happier things; inform us, and prove to us,

that though we are what we are, we may yet, in some way, even in our abasement, even by and through our daily work, be related to the purer existence.

(SPW, pp. 144–145; PPR, I, 361)

Although poetry must have a "message," Clough does not use the word in its modern pejorative sense to indicate a poet's preaching to his readers or giving his readers some facile solution to a pressing immediate problem. The message of the poem is that which gives the reader some new or added insight into his life in general, or into one vital aspect of his life, such as love, death, or friendship. It interprets the significance of all that we do or part of what we do here on earth; it is that which consoles us by showing us how, in our limited and narrow spheres, we still "retain to some central and celestial fact." By defining them in universal terms, the message gives new meaning to those actions, those movements, those ideas that we, in our limited worlds, see only as particulars. Poetry, for Clough, is a criticism of life.

If the poet has the moral responsibility of criticizing life, he must be able to face facts, and the poetry that he writes must be neither remote nor sentimental. The love of truth, as has been seen, was the cornerstone of his entire outlook on life itself, as well as of his criticism. The crucial place it holds in his poetic theory is indicated by his remarks on the age of Dryden and the poetry of Wordsworth. He praises the spirit of Dryden's era as one which had an "austere love of truth," a "righteous abhorrence of illusion," a "rigorous uncompromising rejection of the vague, . . . the merely probable," and a "stern conscientious determination . . . to admit, if things are bad, that they are so." "Such a spirit," he concludes, "claims

more than our attention,—claims our reverence." (*SPW*,
p. 137; *PPR*, I, 351) The veneration for truth also enabled Clough to see, in spite of his great admiration for
Wordsworth, that the poet was guilty of both sentimentality and a certain seclusion from the actual world. "Retiring
early from all conflict and even contact with the busy world,
he shut himself out from the elements which it was his business to encounter and to master. This gives to his writings . . . a certain appearance of sterility and unreality."
Clough also deplores Wordsworth's "mawkish sentimentality": "I find myself a little recoil from the statement that

> *To me the meanest flowers that blow do give*
> *Thoughts that do lie too deep for tears* [sic]."

These faults in Wordsworth's poetry detract from its
essential function, the moral one. "People in busy streets,"
comments Clough, "are inclined I fear to contemn the wild
precepts of the rural moralist." (*SPW*, pp. 119, 120;
PPR, I, 322, 324, 323)

Clough's remarks on the nature, function, and subject
matter of poetry and on the character of the poet must, of
course, be understood in the light of his thought, for they
lose their special meaning when taken from the context of
his idealism and positive naturalism. His admiration of
Wordsworth's "moral" character and poetry and his lack
of praise for Byron reflect the great value he placed on
the belief in God, the essentials of Christianity, and the
native goodness of man; Wordsworth's poetry was able to
"sustain man's moral fabric" and to "originate a spiritual
stability." But his condemnation of Wordsworth for as-
signing too high a place to nature and of Scott for his

"free animal nature" and his commendation of Alexander
Smith and of Dryden and his age for being closer to life
and truth, for rejecting the vague and illusory, illustrate
his realistic determination to see things as they are, including the realization that man has some devil as well as deity
in him. Clough's wish, of course, as we have already seen,
was for man to accept things as they really are rather
than avoid coming to grips with the world by resorting to
conventional behavior, to "mawkish sentimentality," or to
animal actions. He valued the "real" or the "natural" over
the artificial or "unnatural"; and he was especially aware
of the need to keep these separate. While his opposing the
artificial with the natural is logical enough, too often his
opposing the natural with the "unnatural" has not been
understood. Clough shows in his lyrics and satires, especially in *Dipsychus*, that the natural, when it takes extreme forms, is as enervating and debilitating as the artificial. This view is the basis for his rejection of Byron and
Scott and his praise of Wordsworth for exercising a "lordship by right divine over passions and desires." *Moral* or
virtuous must be seen, then, as synonyms for natural, with
the understanding that natural implies a balance of the
idealistic and realistic, of the head and heart; it is, in
short, a positive "naturalism."

The moral basis of his theory led Clough to assign a
prominent role to style, a role as prominent, for instance,
as that which Matthew Arnold gave; for the style, according to Clough, contributed to the moral effect of the poem.
Like Arnold, Clough had a twofold theory of style. On the
one hand, he regards style as the expression or the reflection of the character of the poet; accordingly, he admires
Wordsworth, for example, because his poems "more per-

fectly and exquisitely and unintermittedly express his real meaning and significance and character than do the poems of either Scott or Byron." On the other hand, he regards style as the form itself, that which he calls "that permanent beauty of expression[,] that harmony between thought and word, which is the condition of 'immortal verse' "; (*SPW*, pp. 113–114; *PPR*, I, 317) and it is under this aspect that he discusses the importance of the unity of the poem and the proper place of diction and imagery.

His attitude towards the style as the reflection of the poet's character is convincingly shown by his rejection of poets who are content to imitate rather than labor to develop their own distinctive stylistic note, one which would reflect their essential natures. In his review of Arnold and Smith, he objects to their imitativeness; Smith is too much a disciple of Keats, but there is hope that he is young enough to free himself from his present manner, "which does not seem his simple and natural own." Arnold, too, has failed to develop a style which reflects his particular character; he needs to stop "turning and twisting his eyes, in the hope of seeing things as Homer, Sophocles, Virgil, or Milton saw them"; he needs, instead, to look at things, accept them, and depict them as he sees them. Only in this way will he attain that style uniquely suited to him. (*SPW*, pp. 144, 160; *PPR*, I, 360, 374)

Clough's thoughts on the other aspect of style—the form that the poet gives to his material—are very similar to those of Arnold; both are in complete agreement regarding imagery, diction, and the essential unity of a poem. For both, style in this sense—the permanent beauty of expression, that harmony between thought and word, which is the condition of immortal verse—means not "mere accessories," not "the unneeded but pleasing ornament," but rather the "clearness of arrangement, rigor of development" of the poem. (*SPW*, p. 114; *PPR*, I, 317; preface to 1853 *Poems*) The content of the poem being the most important element, the form (style) must not detract in any way from the message. The sum of the individual parts of a poem must not be greater than the sum of the whole: the diction and imagery must not call attention to themselves, but only contribute to the total impression of the piece.

Clough at all times insists on the importance of not distracting the reader from the central theme. In the course of his review of the poems of Smith he subjects the poet to severe criticism for his excessive fondness for figurative language. By telling his similes and metaphors out as a clerk might sovereigns at the Bank of England, Smith is incessantly calling off "the attention, which the reader desires to devote to the pursuit of the main drift of what calls itself a single poem, *simplex et unum*." In addition, he is so intent on imitating the "exuberant expressions" of the Elizabethans and Keats that he falls at times into the error of using what Clough labels "vicious expressions." After quoting a passage from Smith's *Life-Drama*, he comments: "Our author will not keep his eye steady upon the thing before him; he goes off, and distracts us, and breaks the impression he had begun to succeed in giving, by bidding us look now at something else"; and he concludes with the wish that Smith would learn to use "simpler epithets" and "plainer language." (*SPW*, pp. 165–166; 167; *PPR*, I, 381, 382)

Clough's advice to Smith to acquaint himself with and use models other than the Elizabethans and Keats is his

solution to what he thought the most pressing critical
problem of his time: the lack of unity in the works of the
poets. Finding that Keats, Shelley, and Coleridge, "with
their extravagant love for Elizabethan phraseology," have
led to this "mischief," to excessive imagery and extravagant diction, Clough, concentrating on plainer language,
pointed to the late seventeenth and the eighteenth centuries for guidance. In his lecture on Dryden he remarks
that in Dryden's time people found themselves reading
words "easy at once and graceful; fluent yet dignified;
familiar, yet full of harmony" and that this state of affairs
was due mainly to Dryden himself who "organized the dis-
solving and separating elements of our tongue into a new
and living instrument, perfectly adapted to the require-
ments . . . of the age." (*SPW*, pp. 166, 95; *PPR*, I,
381, 332) He concludes with the lamentation: "Have we
any one who speaks for our day as justly and appropri-
ately as Dryden did for his? Have we anything that will
stand wear and tear as well and be as bright and unobso-
lete in a hundred and fifty years, as Alexander's feast is
today?" (*SPW*, p. 96; *PPR*, I, 333) He repeats this plea
for greater simplicity in his review of Smith and Arnold.
After commenting on Smith's diction, he deplores the
poet's apparent lack of familiarity with an important
period of English language and literature, the period between Milton and Burns. "To write out, as a mere daily
task, passages, for example, of Goldsmith," Clough advises, "would do a verse-composer of the nineteenth century as much good, we believe, as the study of Beaumont
and Fletcher." (*SPW*, p. 168; *PPR*, I, 383)

In the light of these ideas, it would seem at first sight
that the lyric rather than satire would be the genre in

which Clough the poet would most successfully carry out
the ideas of Clough the critic.[4] Certainly, for instance, the
subject matter and the purpose of the lyrics reflect his
critical ideas. The poet, Clough states, should deal with
meaningful subjects, vital in their appeal and timeless in
their interest, and this is what Clough the lyricist does,
treating most often man's relationship to nature, to country, to fellow human beings, and to truth or God. And the
end for which they are written is to provide a criticism of
life, to show that man is capable of living a meaningful
life. In matters of style, too, Clough the poet follows the
dictates of the critic, employing the more traditional
forms, striving for simple diction, and being very sparing
in the use of imagery.[5] Following the recommendations of

4. In making the distinction between Clough's satiric and lyric poems,
I have been guided principally by those qualities that I discuss as characteristic of each genre, especially the tone, purpose, and stylistic manner.
In addition to the three long poems, the *Bothie, Amours,* and *Dipsychus,*
I include in the satiric canon (as distinguished from the lyric) the following "shorter" poems: "Look you, my simple friend, 'tis one of those,"
p. 25; "To the Great Metropolis," p. 48; "Is it true, ye gods, who treat us,"
p. 42; "Duty—that's to say complying," p. 27; "I give thee joy! O worthy
word!" p. 3; "The Latest Decalogue," p. 60; "O land of Empire, art and
love!" p. 64; *"Sa Majesté très Chrétienne,"* p. 69; "I dreamed a dream,"
p. 406; "In the Great Metropolis," p. 91; and *"O qui me,"* p. 106.

5. Although Clough experimented with many different stanzaic forms,
line lengths, and metrical patterns, and it is difficult to understand how
anyone could call him a "rough versifier" and accuse him of lacking poetic
sensibility (Osborne, p. 83), his most successful lyrics are those written in
the "simple," more traditional forms, in which, in conformity with his
critical views, he was able to keep meter, technique, and expression subordinate to theme. His most effective lyrics are written in such regular
forms as the octosyllabic couplet, the tetrameter quatrain, the heroic couplet, the elegiac quatrain, the ballad stanza, and the ode, and his greatest
debt is clearly to Dryden, Pope, Collins, Cowper, Crabbe, the writers in
the "restrained," neo-classic tradition. (See E. N. S. Thompson, "The
Octosyllabic Couplet," *Philological Quarterly,* XVIII, July, 1939, 257–
268.) Of his best lyrics, for instance, three, *"Qua Cursum Ventus,"* "Say
not the struggle nought availeth," and "Put forth thy leaf, thou lofty
plane," are written in iambic tetrameter quatrain or doubled-quatrain;
one, "O stream descending down to sea," is in the ballad stanza form; and

one, "O ship, ship, ship," is in trimeter lines of anapests and iambs. The others are written in longer lines, mostly iambic pentameter: *"Qui Laborat, Orat"* and "The Silver Wedding" in elegiac quatrain; "Farewell, farewell, her vans the vessel tries," "Come home, come home, and where an home hath he," "Come back, come back, behold with straining mast," and "Some future day when what is now is not," in iambic pentameter couplets; and "Why should I say I see the things I see not" and "Easter Day," I and II are irregular odes.

The successful working out of rhythmic phrase and pattern is the characteristic that particularly distinguishes the irregular odes, perhaps the lyric form in which Clough was especially effective. Completely at ease in this genre, he was able to blend idea, emotion, and form in a manner reminiscent of Dryden. "Why should I say I see the things I see not," for instance, captures this spirit. In three stanzas of varying lengths, he makes no attempt to work out any formal pattern. The lines vary from two to seven feet: the first stanza contains twenty-eight lines; the second, nineteen; the third, twelve. The rhyme scheme is irregular, varying from couplets to quadruple rhymes to alternating ones. The entire poem is basically governed by rising rhythm, the poet skillfully employing iambs and anapests to achieve the particular effect he wants at a particular moment. In lines 5 and 6 he uses anapestic measures to portray the hurried, irregular movement done involuntarily: "Shall be hustled and justled about," while in lines 30–32, he uses the regularity of the iambic measure to achieve the effect of loud, blaring music: "One loud and bold and coarse,/ And overpowering still perforce/ All tone and tune beside."

The running images throughout the poem are those of dancing and music, two favorites of Clough. They are particularly suitable in this lyric, whose main concerns are what one should believe and how one should behave. Should one, Clough asks in stanza one, give in to the temptation of simply shutting one's eyes to all the serious problems of the world and "dance" to the superficial and brassy music of the superficial and brassy world; or should one wait it out and keep listening for the "natural" and "innocent" music of his own soul? Stanza two emphasizes the contrast between the two musics; while stanza three, using the minor image of a "palsied nerve," stresses that although one cannot hope simply to do away with the world's music, one can still distinguish the real from the superficial and remain true to the music of his soul.

Diction also plays an important part in unifying the lyric, especially the way in which Clough employs repetition, particularly of such key words as *music, turn, soul*. The opening of the poem illustrates this device, for he plays against each other six different states of being or acting— seeing, being, loving, fearing, dancing, and hearing. In the first four lines *I* is used six times and *not* five, and *see, be, love,* and *fear* are repeated. Yet, there is no effect of excessive repetition, partly because *I* and *not* are unstressed, partly because Clough uses the repetition to emphasize the thought as well as the music. His use of this device in other parts of the poem is particularly effective with *silence* and *silent* in lines 39 and 40, with *listen* in lines 46 and 47, with *turn* in lines 39 and 40, and with the prefix *un* in the penultimate line.

Also impressive is the combination of diction and varied line lengths to achieve onomatopoetic effects. In stanza one, the feeling of being pushed about is reinforced by the *hustled* and *justled* of line 6. A more subtle effect is found in lines 18–21:

> And hand in hand, and heart with heart, with these
>   retreat, advance;
> And borne on wings of wavy sound,
> Whirl with these around, around,
> Who here are living in the living dance!

In these lines the varied line lengths of seven, four, four, and five feet portray the various movements of the dance itself, including the regular rhythm and some variations. The frequent repetitions and the slight use of alliteration also contribute to the musical, repeated movement and sound. Even more felicitous is his use of the single word *whirl* in line 20. While all the other surrounding lines in this series are regularly iambic, line 20 is not. Accordingly *whirl* gets the full accent, its unaccented syllable being absent, and the heavy emphasis approximates both the actual time required by the whirl of the dance itself as well as the effect that the whirling would have in the dance pattern. An equally successful blending of sense and sound is found in stanza two, where Clough distinguishes between the two different musics. The loud, coarse music is conveyed with short, regularly iambic lines, many hard consonants, and telling alliteration. The soft, low music is described in more varied lines, with intermingled iambs, trochees, and anapests, liquid consonants, and, again, effective alliteration.

One further observation might be made on Clough's lyric poetry. His sparing use of imagery has been stressed enough; what has not, however, is the type of image that he used and the way that he used it. Much has been done in recent years to demonstrate the validity of coming to know a poet's ideas by the nature and the use of his imagery. In Clough's case this approach is especially rewarding, for it serves to illustrate still more clearly the essentially moral basis of his lyric poetry and the positive characteristics of his "naturalism." One would expect, for instance, that Clough would employ images that would appeal to "the general wants and ordinary feelings," since he wanted poetry to be more than "mere pastoral sweet piping from the country." It is precisely for this reason that although he did make some use of recent scientific topics and inventions for his imagery, most of the figures in his lyrics come from those aspects and experiences of life common to all men: fighting, dancing and music, nature (particularly the sea), and the Bible. One would expect, too, that he would rely rather heavily on images that reflect growth and movement and serve to contrast the natural with the artificial, since he felt that man was constantly seeking to develop his native goodness and fighting against stifling convention on the one hand and bestiality on the other. Not only does his preference for these "natural" images become understandable, but his emphasis on imagery that contains the element of potential growth or underlying strength also becomes clear. Since he believed that man had the capacity for growth and that eventually this growth and development would come about, he found this type of image most congenial. It is this point that some critics fail to see when they cite *Dipsychus*

the critic, the lyric poet demonstrates the strong influence
that the period between Milton and Burns had on him.
There is some influence by later poets, particularly
Wordsworth and Tennyson, but, on the whole, Clough's
lyrics reflect the critic's praise of neo-classical writing, particularly the qualities of lucidity, plainness, and moral
concern.

But save for some notable exceptions, Clough the lyricist failed to achieve the goal of Clough the critic. It remained for Clough the satirist to do this, and the reasons
for his success in this genre lie ultimately in the poet's
own intellectual and moral attitudes. While both genres
rest on his belief that poetry should be primarily moral-
istic, the satires more clearly reflect this belief and thus
more effectively demonstrate Clough's great concern with
the individual's role in the world and his failure to measure up to an ideal that may be expressed by the term
"organic" or "natural" as opposed to the "mechanic" or
"unnatural." The satires concern themselves much more
specifically than do the lyrics with the "general wants,
ordinary feelings, the obvious rather than the rare facts of
human nature"; they concern themselves more with the
here and now. They are in fact Clough's attempts to "fix a

---

as a poem that illustrates Clough's "submission" to the world. Dipsychus
is plainly not submitting, in the sense that he has been defeated; he, as do
Clough and Clough's Adam, realizes that man is developing and growing
and that the seed eventually becomes the fully grown plant. Finally, one
would expect, since Clough is opposed to "telling similes and metaphors
out as a clerk might sovereigns at the Bank of England," that he would
make certain to have the image be an intrinsic part of the poem rather
than serve as mere "poetic decoration" and that it would contain for the
reader an ethical or moral judgment and not simply be an "attractive
accessory." And so he does. See, in this connection, my "Arthur Hugh
Clough: A Portrait Retouched," *Victorian Newsletter,* No. XV (Spring,
1959), 24–27.

centre around which the chaotic elements of human impulse and desire might take solid form and move in their
ordered ellipses." Also, the satires, unlike most of the
lyrics, contain that harmony of thought and word which
Clough found so essential to poetry. Reflecting the more
vigorous aspects of the neo-classical tradition rather than
the plainness and simplicity found in the lyrics, the satiric
poems are written in that style which reveals the moral
aesthetic so central to his prosodic theory. With its irony,
indirection, and ambiguity, Clough's satire became for
him the most direct and effective way of expressing his
deep concern over man's plight. In his satiric poems,
thought and art became one.

(B) The satiric poetry [1]

From the very start of his career Clough regarded satire
as a medium of reform, and his models seem to be those
satirists who stressed this intent. In a perceptive essay on
Swift, A. E. Dyson has indicated the distinctive marks of
the genre: "Satire, fiercer than comedy in its moral intention, measures human conduct not against a norm but
against an ideal. The intention is reformative. The satirist
holds up for his reader to see a distorted image, and the
reader is to be shocked into a realization that the image is
his own." [2] This description fits Clough's purpose perfectly, for he early stressed the reformative intent of the
satirical method. One of his essays at Balliol was entitled

1. See footnote 4 of the previous section, "The Poetic Theory."
2. A. E. Dyson, "Swift: The Metamorphosis of Irony" in *Gulliver's
Travels: An Annotated Text with Critical Essays*, ed. Robert A. Greenberg, New York, 1961, p. 308.

"The Moral Effect of Works of Satire," in which his main thesis was that true satire was "engendered of love for truth and right." Satire, he wrote, reached its first full development in Rome, under the Imperial tyranny, a time of great and overpowering corruption. "Numbers too careless to heed, and too hardened perhaps to appreciate the more usual and universal admonitions, are by the keen edge of Satire roused to a sense of their folly and baseness. Numbers in whom the most beautiful landscape, the most exalted effort of the painter[']s genius could never excite a sentiment of moral dignity by the bitterness of this more personal poetry may be led to feelings of shame at moral depravity. Numbers again of those who are as yet weakly trembling on the verge and hesitating between the claims of their better mind and the allurements of the general degradation around, would in the Works of Satire find an ally and supporter to the reluctant feelings and doubtful perceptions of conscience which more abstract representations of virtuous sentiments would probably fail to supply." [3] The objects of Clough's own satire are evident in this early essay: "folly," "baseness," "moral depravity," "general degradation," qualities that the poet saw about him. As an "ally and supporter" of the perceptions of conscience, Clough's satiric poems represent a determined attempt to make poetry a vital force for good, to enable man to see the life that befits him when he learns to make full use of his native goodness.

This attitude explains the dominant theme in Clough's satire: his consistent portrayal of the disparity between theory and practice, conviction and convention. "Look

3. See *Checklist,* p. 381, item 15, vii; *SPW,* pp. 63–65. The quotation is on pp. 63–64.

you, my simple friend, 'tis one of those" and "Is it true, ye gods, who treat us" depict the abuse of poetic power for base or insignificant purposes. "To the Great Metropolis" and "In the Great Metropolis" deal with the stultifying influence of laissez-faire. "Duty—that's to say comply- ing" and "I give thee joy! O worthy word!" reveal the debilitating effect of custom and convention; and "The Latest Decalogue," "*Sa Majesté très Chrétienne*," "I dreamed a dream," and "*O qui me*—" have for their cen- tral idea the crippling effects of inaction and mechanical (often hypocritical) behavior, an idea that is also the basis of the longer poems. The underlying motif in all, of course, is the poet's concern to distinguish what ought to be and what really is, the natural from the mechanical; and his satiric art is revealed in the precision with which he is able to do just that.

His employment of imagery is one example of this precision. In general, as already noted, Clough uses imagery sparingly, depending more on direct statement to make his point, and a special significance becomes attached to any image that he employs. It is espe- cially revealing, then, to find that most of the imagery employed in his shorter satiric pieces comes from commer- cial life, even in the poems that deal with other aspects of living. Connected to the imagery, of course, is the choice of language used to depict these, and one of the marks of Clough's satiric poetry is his skill in this area; indeed, his judicious employment of *le mot juste* is only now becom- ing recognized as an intrinsically important characteristic of his poetic art. Most significant, however, is Clough's satiric manner, which reveals most clearly his "consummate management" of words.[4] It is this facet, particularly his manipulation of rhythm and pattern, that marks Clough's greatest departure from his own age and closest connection to ours. This "modern" note may be found in his varied metrical patterns, which are often neither regular nor logically developed; in his varying line lengths, irregular rhymes, and unrhythmical rhythms; his apparent lack of transition between ideas and images; and, most important, his underlying ironic attitude, which makes itself felt most forcefully in the tone of outraged, frustrated sensibility. His satiric poetry represents then, like Eliot's, an attempt to express "those deeper, unnamed feelings which form the substratum of our being, to which we rarely penetrate; for our lives are mostly a constant evasion of ourselves, and an evasion of the visible and sensible world." [5] Like Eliot, too, Clough is interested in presenting the "dream of inaction," [6] and the intense (though repressed) emotion of his satire gives his work a dramatic intensity seldom found in Victorian poetry.

All of these elements, particularly the language and tone, are found in varying degrees in all of Clough's satires, but are especially evident in "Is it true, ye gods, who treat us," one of Clough's most successful satiric pieces.

> *Is it true, ye gods, who treat us*
> *As the gambling fool is treated,*
> *O ye, who ever cheat us,*

4. Houghton, *Studies in English Literature,* p. 44.
5. T. S. Eliot, *The Use of Poetry and the Use of Criticism,* Cambridge, Mass., 1933, p. 155.
6. Lloyd Frankenberg, *Pleasure Dome: On Reading Modern Poetry,* New York, Dolphin Books, 1961, p. 67.

And let us feel we're cheated!
Is it true that poetical power,
The gift of heaven, the dower
Of Apollo and the Nine,
The inborn sense, 'The vision and the faculty divine,'
All we glorify and bless
In our rapturous exaltation,
All invention, and creation,
Exuberance of fancy, and sublime imagination,
All a poet's fame is built on,
The fame of Shakespeare, Milton,
Of Wordsworth, Byron, Shelley,
Is in reason's grave precision,
Nothing more, nothing less,
Than a peculiar conformation,
Constitution, and condition
Of the brain and of the belly?
Is it true, ye gods who cheat us?
And that's the way ye treat us?

Oh say it, all who think it,
Look straight, and never blink it!
If it is so, let it be so,
And we will all agree so;
But the plot has counterplot,
It may be, and yet be not.

Walter Houghton has touched upon Clough's preciseness of diction in his discussion of the poem,[7] pointing out the particular aptness of the poets named—Shakespeare, Milton, Wordsworth, Byron, Shelley—to represent the full range of English poetry; the use of *brain* rather than mind, of *belly* rather than some other word to convey just the right tone of "outraged disillusion"; and the choice

7. Houghton, *SEL*, p. 43; Houghton, pp. 27–30.

of the word *blink* in line 24 to connect it alliteratively and functionally to the "b" alliteration of line 20 and, he might have added, to lines 15, 13, 9, and 28. There are other subtleties of precision that should be noted. A distinction is made between "fancy" and "imagination" in the best Coleridgian fashion, the former being inventive and the latter creative. Even more effective in setting the tone is Clough's phrase "reason's grave precision," in which the word *grave* succinctly indicates the attitude of the poet, who, in spite of the ambivalent ending, clearly regards the emphasis on cold reason and logic as indeed a death-like one. Grave precision is also connected with *brain* and *belly*, words that not only convey the note of vulgarity that Clough wants, but also are associated with the physical, subject to decay and death, rather than the spiritual, the two concepts of poetic inspiration being debated here. These contrasting views are also presented by Clough's emphasis on the word *fame*, a word which instantly brings to mind the fact that the five poets mentioned also were keenly aware of the true nature of fame, especially Milton, to whom Phoebus replied: "Fame is no plant that grows on mortal soil." A close reading and real understanding of what Clough is doing, then, serve to dispel the notion that Clough is inconclusive in his judgments; the fact is that his point is perfectly clear. The only obstacles are those often found in modern poetry—indirection, irony, association rather than direct statement—and when these are overcome, one is impressed by the force with which Clough conveys his central theme.

Forcefulness of purpose is an important element of the sonnet "To the Great Metropolis," written, it would seem, in reply to Wordsworth's "Composed upon Westminster

Bridge," [8] a point that is often missed but which gives an added richness to the poem. That Clough would feel the need to reply is not surprising, since, as we have seen, he felt that Wordsworth often avoided his responsibility as a poet by simply writing about nature rather than concerning himself with the problems of human nature. Precise diction, succinct imagery, and effective rhythm that conveys the attitude of the disillusioned but not uncommitted observer are employed by Clough to reveal his judgment of the city regarded by so many Englishmen as the epitome of civilization. Wordsworth, viewing the city in its somnolent state, could persuade himself, for a moment at least, that a certain majesty prevailed. Clough was not to be taken in, even for a moment. Wordsworth's sonnet, in conventional Italian form, gives a picture of the city at dawn, the mood being one of peace and calm: "Dear God! the very houses seem asleep;/ And all that mighty heart is lying still!" Clough's sonnet, also in Italian form but with a slight variation in the second quatrain, presents a far different picture of the city; the first line, indeed, the first word, sets the contrast of content and tone: "Traffic, to speak from knowledge but begun,/ I saw." Opposed to the peace of the city asleep, we have the characterization of a city dominated by "Traffic," with all the associations that Ruskin was to develop more fully in his famous lecture. Speaking from "knowledge" rather than from Wordsworth's idealistic point of view, Clough goes on to make other contrasts. "Earth has not anything to show more fair," writes Wordsworth; Clough replies by a play

8. I am especially indebted at this point to Richard M. Gollin, "Arthur Hugh Clough: The Formative Years." Doct. Diss. University of Minnesota, 1959, pp. 288ff. See also Chorley, p. 161.

on the last word, personifying Display as one of the characteristics of the great "Capital." Wordsworth sees the city as "bright and glittering" in the smokeless air, and he describes the city in all its *majesty*. Clough opposes these with his condemnation of the city as the "sovereign" symbol of the great and good, with all the glitter, then, coming from its attributes of shiny, hard cash. For Wordsworth's list of the city's sights: "Ships, towers, domes, theatres, and temples," Clough offers his own: "The stranger's fancy of the thing thou art/ Is rather truly of a huge Bazaar,/ A railway terminus, a gay Hotel." And for the climactic effect, he opposes Wordsworth's "mighty heart" with his own judgment: "Anything but a mighty Nation's heart." The cumulative effect of the language taken from commerce, the contrast to the peaceful picture painted by the earlier poet, and the consistent undertone of sincere but suppressed disgust on the part of Clough combine to portray strikingly his satiric condemnation of the city that should be the symbol of "the Great and Good,/ True Royalty, and genuine Statesmanhood,/ Nobleness, Learning, Piety."

The implied condemnation of "To the Great Metropolis" is brought out more forcefully in "Duty—that's to say complying," and the condemnation is extended far beyond London. It is, in fact, Clough's bitterest indictment of his age, an indictment brought out by every artistic mean—content, diction, meter, style. The poem is also significant in that it contains what we can call the "modern" note and thus conveys most clearly Clough's connection to our own time. It consists of forty-four lines of two unequal stanzas, mainly trochaic tetrameter, mostly in couplets, but with every kind of irregularity in line length, meter, and pattern. The irregularity, of course, is functional, indicating the poet's repressed emotion and outraged sensibility; indeed, towards the end the meter seems to break down completely as the poet is reduced to utterances of frustrated denunciations: "Atrophy, exinanition!/ Duty!"; and only after this outburst does he seem to regain control long enough to indicate coherently his denunciation: "Yea, by duty's prime condition/ Pure nonentity of duty!" The final effect is that of a speaker who is "feeling" his thoughts, if not immediately as the odor of a rose, at least as intensively as those two sensibilities can be united.[9]

Specifically, the poem is Clough's portrayal of the Victorian Wasteland, of his unheroic age, in which "stern and prompt suppressing" and "coward acquiescence" are the chief characteristics of life. Elizabeth Drew's description of the people in Eliot's poetry could be applied quite easily to Clough's: "The figures that move about . . . suffer a common impoverishment of emotional vitality. They either live by the 'formulated phrases' of empty social convention and a decadent culture or their lives are purely sordid and sensual." Like Eliot, Clough is able to create "the sense of emptiness, the barrenness, and the consequent frustration of a directionless and counterfeit culture, and the need for a vital purpose and order and wholeness of living." [10] The counterfeit culture is exactly what Clough is condemning: "Duty—that's to say complying/ With whate'er's expected here;" . . . "With the form conforming duly,/ Senseless what it meaneth truly,"

9. Elizabeth Drew, ed., "T. S. Eliot," *Major British Writers,* enlarged ed., 2 vols., New York, 1959, II, 820–821.

10. Drew, p. 823.

and in this culture the formulated phrase—"Upon eti-
quette relying,/ Unto usage nought denying,"—is the
only guide.

There is, however, one significant difference between
Clough's satiric poetry and that of Eliot. In Eliot's poetry
the poet himself appears to be a psychologically displaced
person, who shares with the figures of his poems their
"spiritual coloring." [11] In Clough's poetry this is not so;
Clough always remains apart from his characters, and his
own position is always clear and discernible. The ambiguity of Eliot's poetry holds for his theme as well as his
manner; in Clough's satire the manner is ambivalent, but
the theme never. Like the earlier satirists whom he admired, Clough never obscures the reformative intent.

In this difference lies the key to Clough's satire, for the
quality that distinguishes Clough's satire from the poetry
of the early Eliot is the same one that distinguished his
poetry in his own day. This is, of course, his positive
naturalism. Dissatisfied with the way of human action, he
calls for a clear recognition and restoration of the native
virtues that have become suppressed or smothered by convention. The three long poems—the *Bothie, Amours,* and
Dipsychus—have as their main contrast the natural and
artificial, and the shorter pieces all stress this opposition.
In "Look you, my simple friend, 'tis one of those" the
poet has abused his natural gifts; in "I give thee joy!
O worthy word!" the *real* (i.e., natural) meaning of the
word is emphasized. "To the Great Metropolis," "In the
Great Metropolis," and "*O qui me*—" portray the opposition between the true "realities" and the false attributes of
modern life.

11. Drew, p. 822.

"Duty—that's to say complying" is especially illustrative of his positive naturalism, and particularly so when it is compared to another of Wordsworth's poems, "Ode: Intimations of Immortality," which also has for its theme the difference between what is and what ought to be. Wordsworth's poem stresses the loss of "natural piety" through man's concern to make his whole vocation one of "endless imitation," and in the seventh stanza particularly he stresses those activities which slowly draw man away from "the glory and the dream":

> Behold the Child among his new-born blisses,
> A six years' darling of a pigmy size!
> See, where 'mid work of his own hand he lies,
> Fretted by sallies of his mother's kisses,
> With light upon him from his father's eyes!
> See, at his feet, some little plan or chart,
> Some fragment from his dream of human life,
> Shaped by himself with newly-learned art;
>   A wedding or a festival,
>   A mourning or a funeral;
>   And this hath now his heart,
>   And unto this he frames his song:
>   Then will he fit his tongue
> To dialogues of business, love, or strife;
>   But it will not be long
>   Ere this be thrown aside,
>   And with new joy and pride
> The little Actor cons another part;
> Filling from time to time his "humorous stage"
> With all the Persons, down to palsied Age,
> That Life brings with her in her equipage;
>   As if his whole vocation
>   Were endless imitation.

Like Wordsworth, Clough sees man a prey to the vocation of endless imitation, adjusting his whole existence to "dialogues of business, love, or strife." Principally by the juxtaposition of opposites and the precision of diction he portrays the closing in of the shades of the prison house. "Our birth is but a sleep and a forgetting," Wordsworth writes; Clough states it more bluntly: "Moral blank, and moral void,/ Life at very birth destroyed." Wordsworth mentions festivals and coronals, weddings and funerals; Clough again describes these more tellingly: "On your unknown cousin's dying,/ Straight be ready with the tear"; "Go to church—the world require you,/ To balls— the world require you too,/ And marry—papa and mamma desire you,/ And your sisters and schoolfellows do." Wordsworth may speak of our souls having sight of "that immortal sea"; Clough can find only atrophy in a Bath chair: "Stunt sturdy limbs that Nature gave,/ And be drawn in a Bath chair along to the grave."

The contrast between the two points of view is a significant one. Wordsworth's concern to find "recompense" and his final belief in the philosophic mind are legitimate enough in the context of the ode, but they remain essentially subjective experiences that are in the end meaningful only to Wordsworth himself. Clough's conclusion is that which brings man face to face with reality; like Forster, he possesses the quality that raises him above being a mere moralizer. Clough demonstrates in his satiric writing not only the liberal imagination that can expose the follies and faults of human nature, but also the moral awareness that can make of these experiences a meaningful commentary on life. If the ode is Wordsworth's intimations of immortality, then Clough's poem is an attempt to show that the gleam has always been visionary at best. What man needs to have revealed to him is not an intimation of immortality, but, rather, a clearer understanding of his mortality. Wordsworth's poem reveals his morality; Clough's, his moral realism.

"*Sa Majesté très Chrétienne*," which illustrates even more clearly Clough's "modern" note, his connection with the early Eliot (and, at times, with Browning) is a dramatic monologue that can be called an "ironic summary" of his age. Its modernity is evident in most of its aspects: its form and rhythm, mainly iambic pentameter, but with many irregularities; its tone, which is "unheroic"; its artistic method, which depends on allusion, indirection, association, on psychological rather than grammatical reference; its insight, which depicts accurately and comments penetratingly on the contemporary scene. Like Eliot and Browning, Clough is interested in presenting opposing points of view through a dramatic situation; and his characterization of Louis XV is a masterly portrayal of a personality that embodies most of the elements that he is interested in exploring. Browning's Fra Lippo Lippi comes to mind in the light of Clough's treatment of Louis, who, although having a much different personality, is faced with the same problem that confronts Browning's monk. What do men want? Do they want action or contemplation? Which is better? Pleasure or Duty? Church or State? Sin or Submission? Black serge or Purple gown? Like Lippi and Prufrock, Louis is puzzled by the opposing demands made upon humans by life itself: What would men have?

Clough's speaker is in a confessional, but he is not so

much confessing to another as debating with himself; like
Prufrock, the poem is more interior monologue than con-
fession. The manner is informal, conversational, the ideas
being developed not logically but associatively. "Ah me,"
"Ah, holy father, yes," "Alas," "Ah never, no!" "But,"
"Yet"—these are the connectives between ideas, connectives that indicate the leaps from thought to thought.
Central to the thought are the images employed by the
speaker, the most pervasive one being that of movement.
Louis thinks of the peace he would enjoy if he could "pace
serenely through the sacred fane,/ Bearing the sacred
things before the priest." Instead, like the streets through
which Prufrock must walk are the paths that he must take:

> *Alas, and can it be*
> *In this perplexing labyrinth I see,*
> *This waste and wild infinity of ways*
> *Where all are like, and each each other meets,*
> *Quits, meets, and quits a many hundred times,*
> *That this path more than that conducts to Thee?*

and

> *No, through the long and dark and dismal night*
> *We will not turn and seek the city streets,*
> *We will not stir, we should but lose our way;*

and again

> *If I had so by God's despite been born,*
> *Alas, methinks I had but passed my life*
> *In sitting motionless beside the fire,*
> *Not daring to remove the once-placed chair,*
> *Nor stir my foot for fear it should be sin.*

The king, like Prufrock and Lippi, is well aware of precepts and commandments, especially those that forbid natural actions. Prufrock can hear the mermaids singing; Lippi always sees the garden and God "Amaking man's wife"; Louis, too, is puzzled over the relationship of the "you" and "I":

> Oh, underneath the black and sacred serge
> Would yet uneasy uncontented blood
> Swell to revolt? Beneath the tippet's white
> Would harassed nerves by sacred music soothed,
> By solemn sights and peaceful tasks composed,
> Demand more potent medicine than these,
> Or ask from pleasure more than duty gives?
>
>   *   *   *
>
> Ah, holy father, would I were as you.
> But you, no less, have trials as you say;
> Inaction vexes you, and action tempts,
> And the bad prickings of the animal heats,
> As in the palace, to the cell will come.

Mood, situation, character combine, then, to depict the dilemma of modern man; but it would be a serious mistake to see Louis as the spokesman for Clough (Chorley, pp. 204–206), even to the degree that Lippi, for instance, can be taken as that of Browning. Clough clearly demonstrates his disapproval of Louis who is, like Prufrock, unable to act, unable to make the "you" rise to the surface. If *Maud* is a "little Hamlet," then *"Sa Majesté très Chrétienne"* is a little *Amours*, for the shorter poem is Clough's depiction of one unable to make any kind of compromise with reality. Vacillating between action and inaction, Louis, like Claude of the *Amours*, exists in an intellectual and spiritual vacuum; like Claude, he is an early inhabitant of the Wasteland, a hollow man who deserves little sympathy. Prufrock is the voice of Eliot, who shares with his characters their "spiritual coloring"; Clough, indirect in method but never in theme, asserts his positive naturalism. The poet's own voice, distinct from that of his characters, is heard clearly and strongly, and the distinguishing element is his moral realism.

The qualities that mark the shorter satires are, of course, found in the three long poems, and the progressive development found in them illustrates Clough's increasing awareness of man's dilemma in his own time. The first, the *Bothie*, has not usually been thought of as primarily a satiric poem, and it has seldom been discussed from this particular point of view. Instead, critics have tended to see it from other angles. Some have been concerned with the meter; others have admired Clough's descriptions of natural scenery; and a few have pointed out his skill in delineating character.[12] Most agree that this is the most positive of Clough's long poems, a humorous narrative filled with the joy of eventful living, exhibiting a *joie de vivre* not often found in his work. All this, of course, is true enough; but to ignore the underlying satiric note is to miss the true meaning of the piece and to fail to see Clough's skill as a poetic craftsman. Being the first of his three long poems, the *Bothie* is Clough's initial attempt to develop two important aspects of his satiric art: the thematic opposition of the natural and the artificial and the

12. See Robert Bridges, *Milton's Prosody,* Oxford, 1901, pp. 106–110; Clough's *Poems,* ed. Humphrey Milford, London, 1910, pp. iii–xiv; R. H. Hutton, "Mr. Clough's Long-Vacation Pastoral," *Spectator,* XXXV (January 25, 1862), 104–105; Charles Kingsley, *"The Bothie of Toper-na-Fuosich,"* *Fraser,* XXXIX (January, 1849), 103–110; and W. M. Rossetti, *"The Bothie of Toper-na-Fuosich,"* *The Germ,* I (January, 1850), 36–48.

use of the "innocent" hero. Supporting these with the same techniques that characterize his shorter satires— precision of diction and imagery and effective rhythmic variation—Clough expresses in the *Bothie* the positive naturalism that marks his mature thought and distinguishes his satiric writing.

While the story of the *Bothie* is a simple one, centering about the love affair of Philip ("radical and poet"), a young Oxonian reading in the Highlands, and Elspie, the daughter of the blacksmith David Mackaye, the artistic elements which make up the poem are more complex. For instance, critics have both praised and blamed Clough for his attempt to "anglicize" the meter, but only a few have pointed out the effectiveness of the measure as a satiric device. That the hexameter meter cannot be naturally adapted to the English language is exactly the point that Clough is utilizing with his "anglo-savage" verse form, as he labeled it. As J. M. Robertson (p. 310) has said: "Clough . . . wrote in hexameters not because he thought that special metre, *qua* metre, tractable to serious verse, but because the hexameter was the metre of Homer and Virgil to begin with, and thus afforded endless opportunities for jests of style that would appeal to academic readers." Thus, the meter would be a natural one for what was meant to be a mock-heroic poem, filled with allusions and ironic commentaries; and, in his usual satiric manner, Clough not only used the meter, but, as he warned the reader at the beginning of the poem, introduced every kind of irregularity into it, so that he could enjoy the same freedom of rhythm and variation in tone found in his shorter satires. Certainly the range of satire in the *Bothie*—from the very light to the deeply serious—owes a great deal to this particular aspect of Clough's art.

Even more functional to the fundamentally serious
satiric purpose of the *Bothie* are the images and the diction that Clough employs, two elements of the poem that
up to now have not been sufficiently appreciated. The same
precision of diction that characterizes his shorter satiric
poems is found in the *Bothie*, and it is used with the same
telling effect, particularly in the depiction of character and
the development of imagery. Clough's ability to delineate
character by a choice phrase or even a single word is remarkable. The tutor, Adam, for instance, "White-tied,
clerical, silent," is a contrast to both Lindsay, "lively, the
cheery, cigar-loving Lindsay,/ Lindsay the ready of
speech, the Piper, the Dialectician," and the "great
Hobbes, contemplative, corpulent, witty,/ Author forgotten and silent of currentest phrases and fancies,/ Mute
and exuberant by turns, a fountain at intervals playing."
As Rossetti, who reviewed the *Bothie* favorably in *The
Germ*, pointed out, these people become not mere names
but individuals.

But Clough has a more serious purpose in his delineation of these characters, particularly in respect to the
main ones, Philip and Elspie, and his description of them
is tied in directly with the basic theme of the poem, the
opposition of the natural and artificial. Philip, the Chartist, poet, eloquent speaker, is always described in natural
terms. As Philip is denouncing the artificial Lady Augustas and Floras, Clough characterizes his manner of speaking:

> *But he, with the bit in his
teeth, scarce*

> Breathed a brief moment, and hurried exultingly on with
>   his rider,
> Far over hillock, and runnel, and bramble, away in the
>   champaign,
> Snorting defiance and force, the white foam flecking his
>   flanks, the
> Rein hanging loose to his neck, and head projecting
>   before him.
>
> (Part II, 11. 68–72)

And in another more striking passage, both Philip and
Elspie are described with natural imagery. Philip is the
sea; she the burnie.[13] At first, she is frightened:

> You are too strong, you see, Mr. Philip! just like the sea
>   there,
> Which will come, through the straits and all between the
>   mountains,
> Forcing its great strong tide into every nook and inlet,
> Getting far in, up the quiet stream of sweet inland water,
> Sucking it up, and stopping it, turning it, driving it
>   backward,
> Quite preventing its own quiet running: and then, soon
>   after,
> Back it goes off, leaving weeds on the shore, and wrack
>   and uncleanness:
> And the poor burn in the glen tries again its peaceful
>   running,
> But it is brackish and tainted, and all its banks in dis-
>   order.
> That was what I dreamt all last night. I was the burnie,

---

13. Houghton emphasizes this image for its sexual significance (pp.
107–108), and he is, of course, right; however, this seems much too narrow
an emphasis in the light of Clough's basic philosophical, ethical, and religious outlook.

> *Trying to get along through the tyrannous brine, and*
> *could not;*
> *I was confined and squeezed in the coils of the great salt*
> *tide, that*
> *Would mix-in itself with me, and change me; I felt myself*
> *changing;*
> *And I struggled, and screamed, I believe, in my dream.*
> *It was dreadful.*
> *You are too strong, Mr. Philip! I am but a poor slender*
> *burnie,*
> *Used to the glens and the rocks, the rowan and birch of*
> *the woodies,*
> *Quite unused to the great salt sea; quite afraid and un-*
> *willing.*
>
> (Part VII, ll. 120–136)

But then her true character asserts itself and she realizes
the joy and power of this natural force:

> *But a revulsion wrought in the brain and bosom of*
> *Elspie;*
> *And the passion she just had compared to the vehement*
> *ocean,*
> *Urging in high spring-tide its masterful way through*
> *the mountains,*
> *Forcing and flooding the silvery stream, as it runs from*
> *the inland;*
> *That great power withdrawn, receding here and passive,*
> *Felt she in myriad springs, her sources, far in the moun-*
> *tains,*
> *Stirring, collecting, rising, upheaving, forth-outflowing,*
> *Taking and joining, right welcome, that delicate rill in*
> *the valley,*
> *Filling it, making it strong, and still descending, seeking,*
> *With a blind forefeeling descending ever, and seeking,*
> *With a delicious forefeeling, the great still sea before it;*
> *There deep into it, far, to carry, and lose in its bosom,*

> *Waters that still from their sources exhaustless are fain*
> *   to be added.*
> *   As he was kissing her fingers, and knelt on the ground*
> *   before her,*
> *Yielding backward she sank to her seat, and of what she*
> *   was doing*
> *Ignorant, bewildered, in sweet multitudinous vague emo-*
> *   tion,*
> *Stooping, knowing not what, put her lips to the hair on*
> *   his forehead:*
> *And Philip, raising himself, gently, for the first time,*
> *   round her*
> *Passing his arms, close, close, enfolded her, close to his*
> *   bosom.*
> *   As they went home by the moon, Forgive me, Philip,*
> *   she whispered;*
> *I have so many things to think of, all of a sudden;*
> *I who had never once thought a thing,—in my ignorant*
> *   Highlands.*

                              (Part VII, ll. 153–174)

Behind the delineation of these two "natural characters" lies Clough's essential purpose: the praise of the
natural over the artificial. Philip is the "innocent" hero,
who looks about him and sees the results of attempting to
live only by custom and precept.[14] His very first speech
sets the tone and conveys his attitude; true, there is a
touch of the "eternal political humbug" that Lindsay is
afraid Philip will bring in, but Philip's argument with
society lies deeper than that. After speaking of the "old
fighting" between Scots and English, he remarks:

14. For an interesting commentary on this matter of organic and
mechanical in the Victorian period see Raymond Williams, *Culture and
Society, 1780–1950*, New York, Anchor Books, 1960, esp. pp. 41, 149.

> *We are the better friends, I fancy, for that old fighting,*
> *Better friends, inasmuch as we know each other the*
> *better,*
> *We can now shake hands without pretending or shuffling.*
>
> (Part I, ll. 153–155)

This is the key to Philip's anger and despair, the pretending and shuffling of the world, and to know this is to receive the full import of Clough's satire in the *Bothie*. In
image after image, the poet contrasts the artificial with
the natural, to the denigration of the former. Philip de-
nounces the noble ladies, and Elspie insists that she will not
be a lady. These ladies, says Philip, completely artificial:

> *Seemed like a sort of unnatural up-in-the-air balloon-*
> *work,*
> *(Or what to me is as hateful, a riding about in a car-*
> *riage,)*
> *Utter removal from work, mother earth, and the objects*
> *of living.*
>
> (Part II, ll. 59–61)

What attracted him first to Kate was her utter natural-
ness; Elspie describes her:

> *Katie is good and not silly; tender, but not like many*
> *Carrying off, and at once for fear of being seen, in the*
> *bosom*
> *Locking-up as in a cupboard the pleasure that any man*
> *gives them,*
> *Keeping it out of sight as a prize they need be ashamed*
> *of;*
> *That is the way, I think, Sir, in England more than in*
> *Scotland;*

No, she lives and takes pleasure in all, as in beautiful
    weather,
Sorry to lose it, but just as we would be to lose fine
    weather.

(Part VII, 11. 9–15)

And the poet himself, in one of the most impressive passages of the poem, characterizes the true nature of the
love of Philip and Elspie, who have found the real meaning of joy:

Pass slowly o'er them ye days of October; ye soft misty
    mornings,
Long dusky eves; pass slowly; and thou great Term-
    Time of Oxford,
Awful with lectures and books, and Little-goes and
    Great-goes,
Till but the sweet bud be perfect, recede and retire for
    the lovers,
Yea, for the sweet love of lovers, postpone thyself even
    to doomsday!
    Pass o'er them slowly, ye hours! Be with them, ye Loves
        and Graces!
    Indirect and evasive no longer, a cowardly bather,
Clinging to bough and to rock, and sidling along by the
    edges,
In your faith, ye Muses and Graces, who love the plain
    present,
Scorning historic abridgement and artifice anti-poetic,
In your faith, ye Muses and Loves, ye Loves and Graces,
I will confront the great peril, and speak with the mouth
    of the lovers,
As they spoke by the alders, at evening, the runnel below
    them,
Elspie a diligent knitter, and Philip her fingers watching.

(Part VI, 11. 91–104)

It is the imagery that conveys most forcefully Clough's belief in positive naturalism that is able to overcome pretending and shuffling and at times even to change "the whole great wicked artificial civilised fabric" into its original "Primal Nature and Beauty." The basic imagistic pattern is the opposition of the artificial and natural, the patterned and organic. Objects from nature—flowers, trees, streams, the sea, magnetic attraction—are contrasted to those made by man—architectural structures, trinkets, hot-house plants. "You will not now run after what merely attracts and entices,/ Every-day things highly coloured, and common-place carved and gilded," Adam tells Philip; and Philip himself is constantly making the contrast between the natural and the artificial by means of imagery drawn from nature. He prefers "Roses, violets, lilies," the "out-of-door beauties" to the "exotic plants" with their "dreary botanical titles." To Philip, the truly attractive women are those who are genuinely of the earth, not doll-like: those who abandon "gros-de-naples for plain linsey-woolsey, sandals of silk for clogs"; for these, then, "so feel the sap of existence/ Circulate up through their roots from the far-away centre of all things,/ Circulate up from the depths to the bud on the twig that is topmost!" Contrasted to these natural "out-of-door beauties" are those women who think of themselves in artificial terms, and one of the most successful of Clough's satiric passages in the *Bothie* is that in which Hobbes begins for Philip a treatise upon *The Laws of Architectural Beauty in Application to Women:*

Where shall in specimen seen be the sculliony stumpy-
   columnar,

(Which to a reverent taste is perhaps the most moving
of any,)
Rising to grace of true woman in English the Early and
Later,
Charming us still in fulfilling the Richer and Loftier
stages,
Lost, ere we end, in the Lady-Debased and the Lady-
Flamboyant:
Whence why in satire and spite too merciless onward
pursue her
Hither to hideous close, Modern-Florid, modern-fine-
lady?

(Part II, 11. 147–153)

Philip and Elspie often speak of love metaphorically, in
terms of a growing tree:

Surely the force that here sweeps me along in its violent
impulse,
Surely my strength shall be in her, my help and protec-
tion about her,
Surely in inner-sweet gladness and vigour of joy shall
sustain her,
Till, the brief winter o'er-past, her own true sap in the
springtide
Rise, and the tree I have bared be verdurous e'en as
aforetime:
Surely it may be, it should be, it must be.

(Part IV, 11. 67–72)

And Elspie, too, reflects his ideas:

No, I feel much more as if I, as well as you, were,
Somewhere, a leaf on the one great tree, that, up from
old time
Growing, contains in itself the whole of the virtue and
life of

> *Bygone days, drawing now to itself all kindreds and*
> *nations,*
> *And must have for itself the whole world for its root and*
> *branches.*

(Part VIII, 11. 89–93)

Still another natural image used by Philip is that of the
attraction of magnetic forces. In telling Adam of his meet-
ing with Elspie, Philip writes: "the needle/ Which in the
shaken compass flew hither and thither, at last, long/
Quivering, poises to north." And later he tells Elspie herself: "Yes, I have carried your glance within me un-
dimmed, unaltered,/ As a lost boat the compass some passing ship has lent her,/ Many a weary mile on road, and
hill, and moorland."

The depiction of both the characters and the love of
Philip and Elspie in terms of these natural images is
brought to a climactic finish by one that combines the natural and the supernatural and thus suggests Clough's
own answer to the problem discussed in the poem, an answer further reinforced by the Rachel-Leah allegory
brought in at the end. The image is that of the bridge that
builds itself,[15] the keystone of which is set by a great invisible hand: Elspie tells Philip of her feeling for him:

> *Yes,—I don't know, Mr. Philip,—but only it feels to*
> *me strangely*
> *Like to the high new bridge, they used to build at, below*
> *there,*
> *Over the burn and glen on the road. You won't under-*
> *stand me.*

15. Houghton, p. 106, also makes much of this as a phallic image and
a "Freudian" dream, but, again, the significance goes beyond the merely
sexual.

> *But I keep saying in my mind—this long time slowly*
> *with trouble*
> *I have been building myself, up, up, and toilfully raising,*
> *Just like as if the bridge were to do it itself without*
> *masons,*
> *Painfully getting myself upraised one stone on another,*
> *All one side I mean; and now I see on the other*
> *Just such another fabric uprising, better and stronger,*
> *Close to me, coming to join me: and then I sometimes*
> *fancy,—*
> *Sometimes I find myself dreaming at nights about arches*
> *and bridges,—*
> *Sometimes I dream of a great invisible hand coming*
> *down, and*
> *Dropping the great key-stone in the middle: there in my*
> *dreaming,*
> *There I feel the great key-stone coming in, and through*
> *it*
> *Feel the other part—all the other stones of the archway,*
> *Joined into mine with a strange happy sense of com-*
> *pleteness.*

(Part VII, 11. 57–72)

The answer is that of a compromise, but not in the usual Victorian sense. Philip is not the common Victorian hero who inherits a fortune or becomes a famous author, general, or statesman. He is, in this sense, the "innocent" hero, one who is satisfied with seeking and doing that for which nature meant him, doing the thing he is fit for, "Everyone for himself, and the common success for all, and/ Thankful, if not for our own, why then for the triumph of others,/ Get along, each as we can, and do the thing we are meant for." This naturalism could, of course, be carried to a point that would justify animal-like behavior, but Clough is careful to add that this "isn't likely to be by sitting still, eating and drinking." (Part IX, 1. 72) Philip has found himself; he has found the thing he is fit for, which is hewing, digging, and subduing the earth and his spirit. Again, this last result, that of subduing the spirit, may be seen as unheroic; it is anything but that in Clough's thinking. Indeed, it is heroism of the highest order to realize that they also serve who are able to subdue their spirits and do that which they are fit for. A Prufrock can only talk to himself, while a Philip can act, even if it means going to the Antipodes, for he at least is facing reality, something a hollow man could never do.

In his next long poem, *Amours de Voyage*, Clough explored still further the satiric techniques of form, meter, and characterization that he had employed in the *Bothie*. Unfortunately, his satiric intent was so subtly presented that all of the elements that contributed to the ironic undertone—the epistolary form, the hexameter measure, the unheroic nature of the protagonist, and the inconclusive ending—were not, and still often are not, appreciated or understood.

In April of 1858 Clough wrote to Professor F. J. Child in America, "I do not suppose . . . that anybody finds much natural pleasure in my 5 act epistolary tragi-comedy or comi-tragedy. . . . I think it will have some merit in its conclusion:—but to that also I dare say there will be no affirmative voice but my own." (*Corr.*, II, 546–547; *PPR*, I, 232) In this comment Clough foreshadowed much of the future critical commentary. Because of the epistolary form, the hexameter measure, the unheroic hero, and the anti-climactic climax, most people have not, so it seems, experienced much "natural pleasure" from the poem. Yet, it should be regarded as one of the most notable achieve-

ments of Clough's satiric writing, for it clearly represents
an advance over the *Bothie*. In the *Amours*, Clough weaves
together even more skillfully form and theme, so that the
measure and manner are a vital aspect of his satire; and
he develops in Claude a character who vividly and mem-
orably demonstrates the dangers of misunderstanding the
natural.

The main purpose of Clough in this tragi-comedy is the
exposé of a self-centered prig unable to realize, as does
Philip in the *Bothie*, the necessity of striking a balance
between theory and practice, between independence of and
unity with his fellow men. The protagonist's insistence on
trying to base his life on completely unattainable, unre-
alistic ideals results in his inability to find any happiness
and peace in life. Those critics who have tried to equate
Claude, the protagonist, with Clough himself have revealed
their lack of familiarity with Clough's character; they
have become so involved with the current and inaccurate
traditional view that labels Clough a failure that they have
failed to see that Clough himself was able to do the very
thing that Claude was not. If one sees the *Amours* as the
incoherent and ineffectual wailings of a young Werther
or Childe Harold, then the poem is a failure; if one sees
it as Clough meant it to be seen, a serio-comic analysis of
a Victorian dilettante, then the poem is a triumphant success.

Clough, as has already been noted, wrote the *Amours*
while on vacation in Rome in 1849, when the Roman
Republic was being besieged by French and Neapolitan
forces. Using the action of the siege as background, he
tells the story of Claude, a sensitive, introspective Englishman who dislikes "vulgar society" and hates any kind of

action that brings him into contact with the "vulgar"
world. Claude is forever questioning all things—art, religion, morals. Faced with any sort of choice, he hesitates,
argues every side of every question. Through a friend of
his, he meets the Trevellyns, a nouveau-riche English family traveling in Rome, and falls in love with Mary, one of
the daughters. To escape the siege-ridden city, the Trevellyns leave for Florence, but Claude, horrified at being
asked his intentions regarding Mary, makes an excuse to
remain in Rome. He writes to his correspondent:

> *How could I go? Great Heavens! to conduct a permitted*
> *flirtation*
> *Under those vulgar eyes, the observed of such observers!*
> (Canto III, 11. 278–279)

Soon growing weary of Rome, however, and desiring to be
with Mary again, Claude follows the Trevellyns to Florence. Reaching there, he discovers they have gone on to
Milan. A series of accidents, a missing letter, and various
other circumstances combine to make Claude's pursuit a
fruitless one. Finally, filled with torment and doubt, he
gives up, crediting his ill fortune to the fates. At the end,
we find the hero as we did at the beginning, hesitating,
always questioning, never able to take any definite action.

But to label the ending as inconclusive and anti-climactic is to miss the entire point. Surely to have any other
kind of ending, particularly a happy one, would be to
destroy the artistic integrity of the poem; for Clough's
purpose has been to show the basic inability of a person
like Claude, aspiring somehow to live above the realities of
life, to make any kind of compromise with the "vulgar"
world. Claude has been called by some a Victorian Hamlet,

but the comparison is unfortunate. Hamlet hesitated, it is true, but he was able to come to a decision when the time was propitious; Claude is unable to come to a decision at any time. He is much closer to a more modern figure; Claude is the nineteenth-century counterpart of Eliot's Prufrock; he is what Philip would have become had he been unable to make the necessary compromise between reality and unreality. An early inhabitant of the Waste-land, Claude's world must end with a whimper.

In order to maintain the proper objective approach to both content and character, Clough employed in the *Amours*, quite deliberately, two devices: the hexameter measure and the epistolary method, both of which have the artificial conventionality necessary to insure against the emotional involvement of either reader or author. Clough is always careful not to share with the figures of his poem their spiritual coloring. In the *Amours*, as in the *Bothie*, he employed the hexameter measure because of its satiric possibilities. And it is not only to academic readers, as Robertson suggested, that Clough's skilful playing with the form would appeal; even one superficially familiar with the *Odyssey* or the *Iliad* or the *Aeneid* would realize the incongruity of writing about a self-conscious prig like Claude in the meter used to celebrate the exploits of heroes like Odysseus and Aeneas. One does not have to be very "academic" to see the contrast between either of these and Claude, who wonders if he has the courage to fight:

> *Now supposing the French or the Neapolitan soldier*
> *Should by some evil chance come exploring the Maison*
> *Serny*
> *(Where the family English are all to assemble for*
> *safety),*

> *Am I prepared to lay down my life for the British female?*
> *Really, who knows? One has bowed and talked, till, little*
> *   by little,*
> *All the natural heat has escaped of the chivalrous spirit.*
> *Oh, one conformed, of course; but one doesn't die for*
> *   good manners,*
> *Stab or shoot, or be shot, by way of a graceful atten-*
> *   tion.*
>
> (Canto II, 11. 65–72)

Again, in contrast to both of these courageous and valorous fighters, we find Claude excitedly and fearfully writing of seeing a man killed, or, at any rate, of seeing, as he reports:

> *Passing away from the place with Murray under my*
> *   arm, and*
> *Stooping, I saw through the legs of the people the legs*
> *   of a body.*
>
> (Canto II, 11. 198–199)

It is difficult to believe that Clough, having Claude express these inane sentiments in an imitation of the meter used to recount the glorious episodes of past heroes, was not aiming at a comic effect, especially when this particular "hero" and his ineffectual mutterings are seen against the background of the valiant, though vain, efforts of the small Roman army fighting against the superior French and Neapolitan forces.

The epistolary method achieves the same effects; it enables the reader to maintain objectivity and it serves to emphasize the comic point of view. No one would deny that telling a story through letters is unnatural; since Richardson's Pamela first started scribbling, the critics have pointed out the awkwardness and cumbersomeness inherent in the technique. But, again, it suits Clough's aim admirably; the reader, always aware of the conventionality of the technique, is kept from getting too involved in the character. At the same time, the epistolary method is excellent for an author who wants to portray all facets of his characters, especially the psychological. By having Claude write letters in which he expounds his ideas on every conceivable subject, and by having Georgina, Mary's sister, and Mary herself write letters revealing how they regard Claude, Clough is able to give the reader a fully rounded portrait of his hero.

The descriptions the girls send of Claude are revealing. Georgina sees him as "stupid," as "too shilly-shally"; Mary, who is much more intelligent, sees him as "superior," "selfish," "agreeable, but also a little repulsive." Claude's letters themselves, miniature dramatic monologues as convincing as any of Browning's, present a kaleidoscopic view of all his weaknesses. In just a few lines Claude is able to reveal his complete inability to face any problem—physical, emotional, spiritual. Is he in love? No, he does not think so:

> *Well, I know, after all, it is only juxtaposition,—*
> *Juxtaposition, in short; and what is juxtaposition?*
> (Canto I, ll. 225–226)

Since he admires those fighting for the Roman Republic, why does he not take up arms? He answers his correspondent:

> *Why not fight?—In the first place, I haven't so much as*
> *a musket;*

> *In the next, if I had, I shouldn't know how I should use it;*
> *In the third, just at present I'm studying ancient*
> *marbles;*
> *In the fourth, I consider I owe my life to my country;*
> *In the fifth,—I forget, but four good reasons are ample.*
>
> (Canto III, 11. 68–72)

His only wish is to escape from realities:

> *Hang this thinking, at last! what good is it? oh, and*
> *what evil!*
> *Oh, what mischief and pain! like a clock in a sick man's*
> *chamber,*
> *Ticking and ticking, and still through each covert of*
> *slumber pursuing.*
> *What shall I do to thee, O thou Preserver of Men? Have*
> *compassion;*
> *Be favourable, and hear! Take from me this regal knowl-*
> *edge;*
> *Let me, contented and mute, with the beasts of the field,*
> *my brothers,*
> *Tranquilly, happily lie,—and eat grass, like Nebuchad-*
> *nezzar!*
>
> (Canto III, 11. 207–213)

Not a particularly inspiring ambition, but one well suited to Claude, who applies to himself most often the term "fool."

In the context of Clough's positive naturalism Claude's "foolishness" is symptomatic of a very serious flaw, the inability to accept the natural and to value it over the artificial. He thus needs to be contrasted constantly with Philip, the "innocent" hero of the *Bothie,* whose recognition of the true role that the natural has in life has already been seen. Unlike Philip, who was able to compromise and to find satisfaction in seeking and doing that for which nature meant him, Claude is unable to do so; he can think of the natural only in terms of complete escape from life or of bestiality, the latter serving to connect him with the Spirit in *Dipsychus*. To be natural for him is to lie tranquilly and happily and eat grass. Or he goes to the other extreme, again like the Spirit of *Dipsychus*, and opposes the natural with the artificial. As much as he indulges himself in criticizing the manners and customs of those about him, Claude is himself a victim of the "dialogues of business, love, or strife." Custom, precept, and tradition may be his targets at times, but in the end he is unable to set the real or natural against these artificialities. Claude is, in fact, an early study of the Dipsychian Spirit.

To emphasize the "foolishness" of his hero, Clough keeps placing him in juxtaposition with other figures, usually much more admirable ones. This comparison is done implicitly, as we have already seen, by the use of the hexameter measure. Clough is more explicit, however, having Claude consistently invoke names that immediately suggest glorious deeds and heroic exploits. At various times Claude directly or indirectly invites comparison with such figures as Adam, Vulcan, Apollo, Theseus, Brutus, and Saul, all of whom strongly suggest the difference between Claude's thoughts and acts. He would be a hero, but he is really the Malvolio of the epigraph. He imagines himself with a sword at his side and a battle-horse underneath him; in reality he is an "inverse Saul," seeking a kingdom, but finding "only asses."

Claude's inability to accept fully the natural and reject the artificial is revealed most clearly in his view of the world in which he lives, a view that stresses both its restric-

tive and labyrinthian or maze-like nature. For Claude, as
for the speaker in "*Sa Majesté très Chrétienne*," to whom
he bears a certain resemblance, the world must always remain a "perplexing labyrinth"; and both must conclude:
"We will not stir, we should but lose our way." Indeed, in
the very beginning, the epigraph to Canto I, we are told
that the world, no matter where we turn, "still is the same
narrow crib;/ 'Tis but to prove limitation, and measure a
cord, that we travel." Claude himself tells us that he is
accompanied, wherever he goes, by "a tyrannous sense of
a superincumbent oppression," and he is reluctant to
"Quit our own fireside hopes at the alien call of a neighbour." (Canto I, 1. 36; Canto II, 1. 93) The key to this
aspect of Claude's character, his essentially timid, bour-
geois outlook, is evident almost at once as he tells Eustace
in one of his first letters:

> *I have come into the precinct, the labyrinth closes*
> *   around me,*
> *Path into path rounding slyly; I pace slowly on, and*
> *   the fancy,*
> *Struggling awhile to sustain the long sequences, weary,*
> *   bewildered,*
> *Fain must collapse in despair; I yield, I am lost, and*
> *   know nothing.*
>
> (Canto I, 11. 237–240)

The point that Clough seems to be stressing is that
Claude's view of the world is a self-imposed one, one
brought about by his unwillingness or inability to compromise. Objecting at different times to philistine standards,
Claude himself thinks mostly in terms of these same standards. He is, after all, visiting Italy, doing the grand tour

along with the other tourists. He also is doing what is expected of tourists, visiting the right places, keeping his Murray always at the ready. He even discovers that he enjoys being in the good graces of the Trevellyn family:

> *Is it contemptible, Eustace—I'm perfectly ready to*
> > *think so,—*
> *Is it,—the horrible pleasure of pleasing inferior people?*
> *I am ashamed my own self; and yet true it is, if dis-*
> > *graceful,*
> *That for the first time in life I am living and moving*
> > *with freedom.*
> *I, who never could talk to the people I meet with my*
> > *uncle,—*
> *I, who have always failed,—I, trust me, can suit the*
> > *Trevellyns;*
> *I, believe me,—great conquest,—am liked by the country*
> > *bankers.*
> *And I am glad to be liked, and like in return very kindly.*
> > (Canto I, 11. 213–220)

And in spite of his talk about juxtaposition, he does get serious enough about Mary to follow her at some length. Regardless of his "advanced" ideas about many things, Claude, like the Spirit of *Dipsychus*, does observe the way of the world; he differs only in degree, not in kind, from the others.

That Claude is at times conscious of the dangers of following the artificial is clear enough, for he does occasionally indicate his disgust with it; but since he, like the Spirit, can think only in extremes, he can oppose the artificial only with the negative view of the natural—that is, he is able to equate the natural with either mere physical existence or animal-like behavior. If one cannot fit into the

way of the world, then he must, if he is like Claude, think
in bestial terms:

> *I am the ox in the dray, the ass with the garden-stuff*
> > *panniers;*
> *I am the dog in the doorway, the kitten that plays in*
> > *the window,*
> *On sunny slab of the ruin the furtive and fugitive lizard,*
> *Swallow above me that twitters, and fly that is buzzing*
> > *about me;*
>
> > * * *
>
> *And, to escape from our strivings, mistakings, mis-*
> > *growths, and perversions,*
> *Fain could demand to return to that perfect and primi-*
> > *tive silence,*
> *Fain be enfolded and fixed, as of old, in their rigid em-*
> > *braces.*
>
> (Canto III, 11. 163–166, 170–172)

If one cannot behave "properly," he must go to the other
extreme.

What makes Claude's plight at times a significant one is
that he occasionally seems to be on the verge of reaching
an understanding of the role of the natural in life, of
realizing the "vitality" of those natural forces which he is
constantly denigrating, of sensing the positive quality of
nature and the factiousness of his own point of view. At
one time he is able to tell Eustace:

> *Tell me, my friend, do you think that the grain would*
> > *sprout in the furrow,*
> *Did it not truly accept as its* summum *and* ultimum
> > bonum
> *That mere common and may-be indifferent soil it is set in?*
>
> (Canto III, 11. 40–42)

Here is an instance when Claude, like Philip, seems to grasp something of the satisfaction of "seeking and doing that for which nature meant him." In another letter Claude tells Eustace that, as he paces the streets, he sometimes feels that:

> *All that is Nature's is I, and I all things that are Nature's.*
>
> * * *
>
> *Yea, and detect, as I go, by a faint but a faithful assurance,*
> *E'en from the stones of the street, as from rocks or trees of the forest,*
> *Something of kindred, a common, though latent vitality, greets me.*

(Canto III, ll. 160, 167–169)

Indeed, in his finest moments, which are all too few, Claude can even bring himself almost to the point of self-awareness, of seeing that his view of the natural may in fact be the false one, and it is in these moments that Clough by a number of significant images reveals his hero's dilemma. At one time, for instance, Claude tells Eustace that he feels "like a tree . . . buried under a ruin of brickwork." Another time, using an image meant obviously to contrast with the grain that accepts the soil it is set in, Claude writes: "I, who refused to enfasten the roots of my floating existence/ In the rich earth, cling now to the hard, naked rock that is left me." Mary, too, senses the conflict in Claude, and she can also see the negativism of his approach; echoing his own words, she writes: "She that should love him must look for small love in return,—like the ivy/ On the stone wall, must expect but a rigid and niggard support, and/ E'en to get that must go searching

all round with her humble embraces." (Canto III, 11. 37–
39) Perhaps the image that portrays best Claude's dilemma—his inability to see fully the natural in its positive
sense and his consequent frustration—is one reminiscent
of Eliot's "ragged claws/ Scuttling across the floors of
silent seas." Claude, too, thinks in terms of the sea:

> *So we cling to our rocks like limpets; Ocean may*
> *bluster,*
> *Over and under and round us; we open our shells to*
> *imbibe our*
> *Nourishment, close them again, and are safe, fulfilling*
> *the purpose*
> *Nature intended,—a wise one, of course, and a noble, we*
> *doubt not.*
>
> (Canto II, 11. 44–47)

Here, then, is the fatal flaw of Claude, revealed in all its
depth. He is incapable of understanding nature, mistaking mere animal-like existence, exemplified by the limpet,
for purposeful "natural" growth, exemplified by the
grain. (In *Dipsychus* Clough uses for a climactic image
"the golden leas.") Essentially negative, Claude thus rejects one source from which he could, indeed, gain some of
the "vitality" he so badly needs. The mermaids will not
sing to Claude, for he is too much aware of human voices.
Unlike Philip, he is unable to think of the natural as either
a source of strength or as the means for finding the thing
he is fit for. Unlike Philip, again, who knew the value of
faith and love as well as knowledge, Claude cannot bring
himself to that state of innocence in which he can see the
positive value of the natural over the artificial. His refusal
to compromise results in his defeat.

Behind this study of Claude's failure lies Clough's own rejection of the artificiality of the world which Claude and the others inhabit, a world in which custom and convention are the standards of morality and behavior. In the world of the *Amours*, as depicted by Clough, there is very little difference in the behavior of Government, Church, and Family. All are ruled by "reverent worship of station"; all are eager to "perform the old ritual service of manners." Artificiality governs all; the natural has no place.

Clough's objections to this world ruled by the values of the middle-class family, a philistine world with cash-nexus relationships, are developed by the events which form the social, political, and religious background. The Italians, a "nice and natural people," are being defeated by the Aristocratic nations, the Barbarians of Arnold, who reverence tradition, custom, and ritual. The Church, too, demands these same responses, and this is why Clough can say that the Christian faith is not in Rome. This is also why he can equate Church and Army: "Priests and soldiers:—and, ah! which is worst, the priest or the soldier?" He can also equate Tourist and Church: "Waiting till Oudinot enter, to reinstate Pope and Tourist"; for Society, like the Church and the Aristocrats, has put a premium on "the old ritual service of manners."

The Trevellyns, of course, are the prime example of this philistine world. With their seven-and-seventy boxes, talking of the A.'s and the W.'s, having about them the taint of the shop, middle-class people, country bankers, grating the ear with the slightly mercantile accent, they demand their shilling's worth, "their penny's pennyworth even." At the very least, they demand "good manners" in everything. Georgina insists that Claude go through the proper procedure of making his proposal to Mary. Vernon is a favorite, no doubt, because he does everything properly, from dancing well to tying Susan's bonnet. Even Mamma keeps up with the expected "refinement" by affecting the blue, talking often of poets, quoting Childe Harold. Bound by the reverent worship of station, determined to observe the artificial letter rather than the natural spirit, all the characters in the *Amours*, members of Church, State, and Family, represent in microcosm the macrocosmic way of the world. Claude, though the main character, is by no means the only foolish one of the *Amours*.

The *Amours*, then, is Clough's second long assay into the satiric form, and what has deprived it of its rightful praise is that its purpose and techniques have been misunderstood. The poem is not the autobiography of a doubter written in a poor imitation of classic meter. It is a serious theme treated in a satiric manner, and the appeal of the poem lies in the universality of this theme: the conflict between absolute idealism and practical realism. Claude is, in this sense, Everyman, who must face the problem of reconciling one's theories with the harsh realities of everyday practices. His failure, dramatized in terms of his conflict over the natural and artificial, is his refusal to make any kind of compromise. He thus exists in an intellectual and spiritual vacuum, and becomes the object of comic laughter. Employing the techniques and approach that he had tried in some of his shorter pieces and in the *Bothie*, Clough reasserted in the *Amours* his belief in man's need to effect a compromise between theory and practice, the natural and the artificial, if he is to sur-

vive the division of his age. In the third of his long satiric
poems he was to portray most strikingly of all the dilemma
faced by one in search of this compromise.

Dipsychus represents for Clough the culmination of
various aspects of his thought and art. In the former, it
represents his most deliberate statement on the question of
man's role in life. Often misunderstood, Dipsychus, the
protagonist, is not another Faust or Claude; he is not even
the exact opposite of the Spirit. Instead, he represents the
compromise that Clough saw so necessary to make. In
terms of the natural as opposed to the artificial, Dipsychus
is an example of one who, although unable to act immediately, has come to realize the full import of finding the
proper relationship between the two. Unlike the Spirit,
who knows only the extremes of both, Dipsychus learns
and comes to value the importance of subduing one's spirit
and finding the thing he is fit for. Unheroic in conventional terms, he is anything but that in Clough's; for he
at least comes to face reality and acts on his beliefs. In
terms of Clough's art, *Dipsychus* represents the blending
of the two major strains of his poetry. With its mixture of
lyricism and satire, the emphasis always being on the latter, its shifting styles and points of view, its rapid changes
of mood, its skilful incorporation of all the elements
found in his best satiric poetry, including such "modern"
ones as vulgar images, slang, and foreign phrases, *Dipsychus* is Clough's most ambitious and successful long
work. If he had written only this poem and nothing else,
he would have to be reckoned with in any account of Victorian poetry.

The form and metrical qualities of *Dipsychus* have a
modern ring to them that is impressive in its total effect.

All the elements by which the poetry of the early twentieth century has been characterized are found in it: the juxtaposition of sensuous lyricism and cacophonous satire; the presence of colloquial diction, often becoming slang; the use of allusion, innuendo, and suggestion, even to the employment of foreign words and phrases; and the consistent treatment of heroic matters in an ironic, unheroic manner.

The metrics of *Dipsychus* demonstrate Clough's mature satiric art, for they are implicitly functional. The opposition of the two characters, for instance, is heightened by the manner in which they speak; Dipsychus most of the time is given the more regular lyrical lines, which help to illustrate both his idealism and his subjective questioning of all things. "O let me love my love unto myself alone," "How light we go, how soft we skim," the long blank verse speech beginning "The Law! 'twere honester, if 'twere genteel," are all the more meaningful as lyrical utterances because of the contrast they present with the more irregular, more masculine, often vulgar and coarse lines of the Spirit, "the persecuting voice" that haunts Dipsychus. At times, the tone of the Spirit's lines, characterized by colloquial, slangy diction and comic rhymes, reminds one of Byron:

> *You'd like another turn, I see.*
> *Yes, yes, a little quiet turn.*
> *By all means let us live and learn.*
> *Here's many a lady still waylaying,*
> *And sundry gentlemen purveying.*
> *And if 'twere only just to see*
> *The room of an Italian* fille,
> *'Twere worth the trouble and the money.*

You'll like to find—I found it funny—
The chamber où vous faites votre affaire
Stand nicely fitted up for prayer;
While dim you trace along one end
The Sacred Supper's length extend.
The calm Madonna o'er your head
Smiles, col bambino, *on the bed*
Where—but your chaste ears I must spare—
Where, as we said, vous faites votre affaire.
They'll suit you, these Venetian pets!
So natural, not the least coquettes—
Really at times one quite forgets—
Well, would you like perhaps to arrive at
A pretty creature's home in private?
We can look in, just say good night,
And, if you like to stay, all right.
Just as you fancy—is it well?

(Scene IIA, 11. 98–122)

Or:

(Bravo, bravissimo! this time though
You rather were run short for rhyme though;
Not that on that account your verse
Could be much better or much worse.)

(Scene IV, 11. 78–81)

And:

The Devil! we've had enough of you,
Quote us a little Wordsworth, do!
Those lines that are so just, they say:
'A something far more deeply' eh?
'Interfused'—what is it they tell us?
Which and the sunset are bedfellows.

(Scene IV, 11. 290–295)

At other times, the Spirit can become very serious, and the
tone is closer to the Wasteland genre; without sacrificing
any of the satiric elements that characterize his lines, he
can bring Dipsychus face to face with ideas that have a
ring of righteousness to them:

> *O yes! you thought you had escaped, no doubt,*
> *This worldly fiend that follows you about,*
> *This compound of convention and impiety,*
> *This mongrel of uncleanness and propriety.*
> *What else were bad enough? but, let me say,*
> *I too have my* grandes manières *in my way;*
> *Could speak high sentiment as well as you,*
> *And out-blank-verse you without much ado;*
> *Have my religion also in my kind,*
> *For dreaming unfit, because not designed.*
> *What! you know not that I too can be serious,*
> *Can speak big words, and use the tone imperious;*
> *Can speak, not honeyedly of love and beauty,*
> *But sternly of a something much like duty?*
> *Oh, do you look surprised? were never told,*
> *Perhaps, that all that glitters is not gold?*
> *The Devil oft the Holy Scripture uses,*
> *But God can act the Devil when He chooses.*
> *Farewell! But,* verbum sapienti satis—
> *I do not make this revelation gratis.*
> *Farewell; beware!*
>
> (Scene XI, ll. 47–67)

The antithetical logic, the colloquialisms, the coarse
imagery are all intrinsically those of the Spirit's speeches,
but these are sometimes mingled with a Polonius-like
solemnity that give to his lines a quality that is unique to
Clough's poetry in this period.

Like his speeches, the Spirit is a mixture of these two

strains, the vulgar and the over-solemn. He represents not only the way of the world, the believer in custom and convention, but also the extreme form of "naturalism," an example of what can result when the proper relationship between the artificial and the natural is not clearly understood. The Spirit, then, is a representative of the two extremes which any man must avoid: "This compound of convention and impiety,/ This mongrel of uncleanness and propriety." He seems to uphold either the freest licence in all things—sex, religion, politics—or the utmost propriety. For him no compromise is possible. Thus we find him at the very beginning advising Dipsychus to abandon himself to the pleasures of the moment, not to hesitate to pick up and have his affair with the girls just waiting for such happenings: " 'Tis here, I see, the custom too/ For damsels eager to be lovered/ To go about with arms uncovered." When Dipsychus resists: "Could I believe that any child of Eve/ Were formed and fashioned, raised and reared for nought/ But to be swilled with animal delight/ And yield five minutes' pleasure to the male," the Spirit taunts him, comparing him to such chivalrous and chaste "lovers" as Joseph and Don Quixote. He insists on the reality of the present, in contrast to such illusory abstractions as beauty and truth:

> *These juicy meats, this flashing wine,*
> *May be an unreal mere appearance;*
> *Only—for my inside, in fine,*
> *They have a singular coherence.*

> *This lovely creature's glowing charms*
> *Are gross illusion, I don't doubt that;*

> But when I pressed her in my arms
> I somehow didn't think about that.
>   (Scene IV, 11. 105–112)

When this fails to impress Dipsychus, the Spirit reverts to his other nature and insists on strict observation of custom. Here, then, is "artificiality" with a vengeance. If Dipsychus does not want to pick up one of the girls of the street, then he must learn to appreciate those of high society:

> Those lovely, stately flowers, that fill with bloom
> The brilliant season's gay parterre-*like room*,
> Moving serene yet swiftly through the dances;
> Those graceful forms and perfect countenances,
> Whose every fold and line in all their dresses
> Something refined and exquisite expresses?
>   (Scene III, 11. 83–88)

In the same spirit he insists that Dipsychus fight a duel, get married, enter the law or the church:

> You'll go to church of course, you know;
> Or at the least will take a pew
> To send your wife and servants to.
> Trust me, I make a point of that;
> No infidelity, that's flat.
>   (Scene VIII, 11. 60–64)

And again:

> Of course you'll enter a profession;
> If not the Church, why then the Law.

> *By Jove, we'll teach you how to draw!*
> *Once in the way that you should go,*
> *You'll do your business well, I know.*
> (Scene VIII, 11. 109–113)

Finally, in a climactic half-lyrical, half-satiric passage, the Spirit relentlessly pursues Dipsychus with a series of logical reasons for pursuing the way of the world:

> *Submit, submit!*
> *For tell me then, in earth's great laws*
> *Have you found any saving clause,*
> *Exemption special granted you*
> *From doing what the rest must do?*
> *Of Common Sense who made you quit,*
> *And told you, you'd no need of it,*
> *Nor to submit?*
>
> *To move on angels' wings were sweet;*
> *But who would therefore scorn his feet?*
> *It cannot walk up to the sky;*
> *It therefore will lie down and die.*
> *Rich meats it don't obtain at call;*
> *It therefore will not eat at all.*
> *Poor babe, and yet a babe of wit!*
> *But Common Sense? Not much of it,*
> *Or 'twould submit.*
>
> *Submit, submit!*
> *As your good father did before you,*
> *And as the mother who first bore you!*
> *Oh yes! a child of heavenly birth!*
> *But yet it was pupped too on earth.*
> *Keep your new birth for that far day*
> *When in the grave your bones you lay,*

All with your kindred and connection,
In hopes of happy resurrection.
But how meantime to live is fit,
Ask Common Sense; and what says it?
Submit, submit!

'Tis Common Sense and human wit
Can find no higher name than it.
Submit, submit!

O I am with you, my sweet friend,
Yea, always, even to the end.

    (Scene X, 11. 163–196)

Dipsychus, however, is not to be deluded, and Clough again depicts the "innocent" hero who insists on finding the compromise between the natural and the artificial, convention and impiety. Having characteristics of two earlier protagonists, Philip and Claude, Dipsychus is at once hesitant and resolved, weak and strong. He is, in short, human, with different moods at different times. But he is by no means to be seen as another Claude, unable to decide what to do and how to go about doing it. On the contrary, he is much more like Philip, who in his own quiet, unheroic manner did find that which nature meant for him to do. In his desire to be honest with himself, on calling for the true recognition of man's nature in terms of his emotions and desires, on resisting the cynicism of the Spirit and insisting on the existence of idealism in the world, and on his refusal to take the easy way out of his dilemma, by either becoming another Spirit or another Claude, Dipsychus gains our admiration. In this respect, Dipsychus resembles Hamlet, for they both come to a better understanding

of themselves and the world. Claude, as we have seen, is
like Prufrock; Dipsychus, on the other hand, a moral
realist, is more like Philip, who comes to the realization
that at the proper time one must stop theorizing and act.
Thus, Dipsychus's compromise is not a defeat but a vic-
tory. He gives in not in a spirit of submission:

> *Not for thy service, thou imperious fiend,*
> *Not to do thy work, or the like of thine;*
> *Not to please thee, O base and fallen spirit!*
> *But One Most High, Most True, whom without thee*
> *It seems I cannot.*
>
> (Scene XII, 11. 32–36)

The conflict in Dipsychus is developed by Clough
mainly through meter, allusion, and imagery, employed in
the "modern" manner we have seen in his other satire. In
Dipsychus's moments of disgust, his lines have the same
harsh tone of those of the Spirit, and they also contain the
same colloquial diction and exaggerated beat of the
Spirit's lines:

> *Ring, ting; to bow before the strong,*
> *There is a rapture too in this;*
> *Speak, outraged maiden, in thy wrong*
> *Did terror bring no secret bliss?*
> *Were boys' shy lips worth half a song*
> *Compared to the hot soldier's kiss?*
> *Work for thy master, work, thou slave*
> *He is not merciful, but brave.*
> *Be't joy to serve, who free and proud*
> *Scorns thee and all the ignoble crowd;*
> *Take that, 'tis all thou art allowed,*
> *Except the snaky hope that they*

May some time serve, who rule to-day,
When, by hell-demons, shan't they pay?
O wickedness, O shame and grief,
And heavy load, and no relief!
O God, O God! and which is worst,
To be the curser or the curst,
The victim or the murderer? Dong
Dong, there is no God; dong!
                    (Scene V, 11. 73–92)

In his moments of aspiration, he utters some strikingly
beautiful blank verse passages that reveal his ideals and
hopes and offer an effective contrast to his other lines. In
Scene X, for instance, "The Piazza at Night," Dipsychus
communicates his feelings of peace:

There have been times, not many, but enough
To quiet all repinings of the heart;
There have been times, in which my [tranquil] soul,
No longer nebulous, sparse, errant, seemed
Upon its axis solidly to move,
Centred and fast; no mere chaotic blank
For random rays to traverse unretained,
But rounding luminous its fair ellipse
Around its central sun.
                    O happy hours!
O compensation ample for long days
Of what impatient tongues call wretchedness!
O beautiful, beneath the magic moon,
To walk the watery way of palaces!
                    (Scene X, 11. 1–13)

The ambivalence is further heightened by Clough's use
of one of the favorite devices of modern poets, allusive references to heroic individuals. The Spirit's disdainful com-

parison of Dipsychus with Don Quixote and Joseph have already been mentioned. Dipsychus himself is constantly contrasting or comparing his own behavior with other figures, Napoleon, Hamlet, Hotspur, John, and Samson, sometimes directly, sometimes more obliquely:

> *I see Napoleon on the heights, intent*
> *To arrest that one brief unit of loose time*
> *Which hands high Victory's thread; his Marshals fret,*
> *His soldiers clamour low: the very guns*
> *Seem going off of themselves; the cannon strain*
> *Like hell-dogs in the leash. But he, he waits;*
> *And lesser chances and inferior hopes*
> *Meantime go pouring past. Men gnash their teeth;*
> *The very faithful have begun to doubt;*
> *But they molest not the calm eye that seeks*
> *'Midst all this huddling silver little worth*
> *The one thin piece that comes, pure gold.*
>
> (Scene IX, 11. 45–56)

His references to Hamlet and Samson are less direct, but none the less effective in revealing his mood of the moment. After his thoughts on Napoleon, he wonders if he will be ready for the right moment when it comes:

> *Yet if the occasion coming should find* us
> *Undexterous, incapable?*
> (Scene IX, 11. 64–65)

At another time he thinks of the difference between the present and the past:

> *And am not I, though I but ill recall*
> *My happier age, a kidnapped child of Heaven,*
> *Whom these uncircumcised Philistines*

> *Have by foul play shorn, blinded, maimed, and kept*
> *For what more glorious than to make them sport?*
> *Wait, then, wait, O my soul! grow, grow, ye locks,—*
> *Then perish they, and if need is, I too.*
>   (Scene XII, 11. 77–83)

The last thought is important, for it demonstrates still another difference in the poetic methods of Eliot and Clough. Prufrock is always making these contrasts to indicate the weakness of his spiritual being; Dipsychus is not so consistent in this attitude. At times he does reflect this aspect, but in other instances he reveals his belief that he will at least approach the heroic proportions of these figures. Like Samson, he will let his locks grow and, if need be, perish in the act of overcoming his enemies. Like Hamlet, he will be ready to act; when the occasion does come, it will find him dextrous and capable.

The most effective of Clough's revelatory devices, however, is imagery, and once again, as in the *Bothie* and the *Amours*, there is the contrast of the natural with the artificial, with the reactions of the characters to one or the other being the chief means by which they are to be judged. The Spirit, that compound of convention and impiety, insists on the strict observance of custom and conventionality; in contrast, Dipsychus, the moral realist, viewing things from his attitude of positive naturalism, insists on the superiority of the natural over the artificial. Unlike Claude and the Spirit, who can think of the natural only in negative terms, Dipsychus thinks of it in more positive terms. He does not want to change man; he wants only to have men change.

The contrast between the two is seen in terms of the imagery from the very beginning of the poem. Having

failed to convince Dipsychus of the need to indulge in an
affair, the Spirit changes his tactics and points out the
advantage of going into society, where, of course, everything is completely artificial: "If the plebeian street don't
suit my friend,/ Why he must try the drawing room, one
fancies." The Spirit would not, one sees, be the least upset
by the room where "the women come and go/ Talking of
Michelangelo." And the Spirit, unlike Philip, sees nothing wrong with those "artificial Lady Augustas and
Floras" who make up this society:

> *O really, your discernment makes me smile—*
> *Do you pretend to tell me you can see*
> *Without one touch of melting sympathy*
> *Those lovely, stately flowers, that fill with bloom*
> *The brilliant season's gay parterre-like room,*
> *Moving serene yet swiftly through the dances;*
> *Those graceful forms and perfect countenances,*
> *Whose every fold and line in all their dresses*
> *Something refined and exquisite expresses?*
> *To see them smile and hear them talk so sweetly*
> *In me destroys all grosser thoughts completely.*
>
> (Scene III, 11. 80–90)

In the same way, as has already been pointed out, he finds
it absolutely imperative that Dipsychus fight the duel, go
to church, get married, in short, to rule his conduct simply
by the case. The point is, of course, that the Spirit recognizes nature, but he insists that it be buried: "To give
up nature's just what wouldn't do./ By all means keep
your sweet ingenuous graces,/ And use them for the
proper time and places." His conclusion follows logically:
"One shouldn't analyse the thing too nearly;/ The main
effect is admirable clearly./ Good manners, said our great

aunts, next to piety ;/ And so, my friend, hurrah for good
society."

Dipsychus, who remains unconvinced of the need for
"good" society, resorts to appropriate imagery to convey
his distrust:

> *To herd with people that one owns no care for;*
> *Friend it with strangers that one sees but once;*
> *To drain the heart with endless complaisance;*
> *To warp the unfashioned diction on the lip,*
> *And twist one's mouth to counterfeit; enforce*
> *Reluctant looks to falsehood; base-alloy*
> *The ingenuous golden frankness of the past;*
> *To calculate and plot; be rough and smooth,*
> *Forward and silent; deferential, cool,*
> *Not by one's humour, which is the safe truth,*
> *But on consideration—*
>
> (Scene III, 11. 34–44)

He does, it is true, reflect in his weaker moments the
Claude-like aspect of his nature, which Clough has him
display with some Prufrockian images: "Aimless and
hopeless in my life I seem/ To thread the winding byways
of the town,/ Bewildered, baffled, hurried hence and
thence,/ All at cross-purpose ever with myself,/ Unknow-
ing whence from whither." Or again, when he wishes to
eliminate "This interfering, enslaving, o'ermastering
demon of craving" within himself. But in his better, more
"natural," "innocent" moments, he indicates through his
imagery his awareness of the moral reality that must
guide one's life. In answer to the Spirit's demands that
conduct must be ruled by artificial conventionalities, Dipsychus laments that often "pallid hotbed courtesies"
must "forestall/ The green and vernal spontaneity,/ And

waste the priceless moments of the man/ In regulating manner." He consistently contrasts restricted, regulated objects with free and natural ones. The "dashing stream" that "Stays not to pick up his steps among the rocks,/ Or let his water-breaks be chronicled" is opposed to the more rigid form: "to live now/ I must sluice out myself into canals,/ And lose all force in ducts." The organic view of the world is seen in juxtaposition to that of the world as a "vast machine," in which "No individual soul has loftier leave/ Than fiddling with a piston or a valve." In his finest moments Dipsychus identifies himself with those free, unrestricted forms of nature that have no mechanical identification: a bud that may yet "bloom freely in celestial clime," a dashing stream, stars, the "roseate westward sky," the Alps, the winds, the sea, the fruitful champaign. Again, carried to its logical conclusion, this identification with the natural could well result in an uninhibited, unrestricted code of behavior, but Dipsychus, like Philip, is not to be seduced by this thought. When he at last gives in to the Spirit, he does so with the knowledge that "we have knowledge wiser than our fears" and "in all these things we—'tis Scripture too—/ Are more than conquerers, even over you." Claude, we remember, advised his friend Eustace to seek knowledge, and leave "mere" faith and love with the chances. Dipsychus, like Philip and like Clough himself, has come to know that all three are important.

There is one other aspect of Dipsychus's "surrender" that needs to be emphasized, one that involves his attitude towards the future. Dipsychus, unlike Claude, realizes the need for flexibility and growth of the human spirit. With his realistic attitude and his recognition of the positive qualities of naturalism, he comes to know that to face the truth is to have change, change that often involves the deepest kind of pain. "Was any change,/ Any now blest expansion, but at first/ A pang, remorse-like, shot to the inmost seats/ Of moral being?" But he is ready and willing to act on his newly-found knowledge, and thus his compromise is one that is both ennobling and fruitful. It is in the light of this positive naturalism that we can gain the full import of the passage that ought to be regarded the crux of the entire poem, the central thought of which contains the key to Clough's satiric art and thought:

> *What we call sin,*
> *I could believe a painful opening out*
> *Of paths for ampler virtue. The bare field,*
> *Scant with lean ears of harvest, long had mocked*
> *The vext laborious farmer. Came at length*
> *The deep plough in the lazy undersoil*
> *Down-driving; with a cry earth's fibres crack,*
> *And a few months, and lo! the golden leas,*
> *And autumn's crowded shocks and loaded wains.*
>   (Scene X, ll. 34–42)

Like Keats's *Ode to Autumn*, these lines reflect Clough's full recognition of man's need for both joy and grief and his spiritual capacity to encompass both.

The qualities that mark Clough's satires illustrate the nature of his satiric achievement. If we postulate effectiveness of communication, intensity of tone, depth of insight, and sharpness of vision as attributes of successful satire, then Clough's place as a satiric artist is assured. With his preciseness of diction, scrupulous employment of imagery, skilful handling of rhythm and meter, and "modern" tone, he conveys distinctly and with considerable force the reformative intent that is the basis of his satiric writing. When to these verbal qualities are added those of his own character—his positive naturalism and "liberal" thought —we can see why his satire would appeal to modern man, who, caught in the terrible division of his age, respects and responds to poetry that speaks decisively and unashamedly in praise of the great and good, of nobleness, learning, and piety; in short, of man's native goodness, his innocence.

❧ Conclusion

It is always difficult to overcome tradition, but it is possible to do so; and in Clough's case there is cause for believing that the traditional view of him as a might-have-been, as one whose name is always associated with failure, will be overcome. And this would apply to the view of Clough as thinker as well as artist, for his thought is the basis of his art. To understand his artistry and to appreciate fully his artistic success, we must understand the positive direction of his thought, especially his commitment to life; his recognition of the dignity of the human spirit, with its capacity for growth and service; his belief in innocence; and his strong faith in truth or God. At the core of Clough's thinking is an intellectual and moral toughness that up to now has not been fully recognized; and, since his poetry is a moral poetry, this lack of complete understanding of his ideas has resulted in the failure to appreciate the full extent of his poetic achievement. "Say not the struggle nought availeth," "Some future day," "Hope evermore and believe," "It fortifies my soul to know," "Christ is yet risen,"—all of these are not mere platitudes, but affirmations of faith, and, to Clough, important enough to form the basis of a poetic theory as well as a way of life. To condemn Clough as man and thinker is to condemn him as artist, for the two cannot be separated; once this fact is recognized, and the strength of his moral conviction seen, the tradition will die.

Desmond MacCarthy, a critic with some idea of Clough's real strength, called him a man of strong will, who "was more like a muscle-bound athlete than a weakling in respect of will power." [1] His statement, both right and wrong, helps to bring into focus the reasons for the misunderstandings that have arisen. MacCarthy is right in his recognition that Clough did have definite ideas about the important intellectual and moral areas of life and that he did arrive at certain conclusions which he supported wholeheartedly in daily living. Guided especially by his belief in man's native goodness and by the conviction that although "born to human trouble" he was also destined for some "diviner lot," Clough was not without hope; despite Houghton's conclusion (p. 223), Clough's vision was not "simply a quiet joylessness as of a burden borne without complaint and without hope." The real strength of purpose and the determination of Clough are obviously still unrecognized.

Writing to Charles Norton, Mrs. Clough commented on her husband's moral and intellectual firmness: "Morally

1. Desmond MacCarthy, *Portraits,* London, 1931, p. 64.

he seemed, to me at least, quite perfect except that he would not work according to his strength, but according to his will and nothing could turn him from it. But intellectually, it was impossible not to see the growth of his mind—it was not finished—it was not even expressed and it is grievous to me that it was so." *(Corr.,* II, 614) Evident in this statement is Mrs. Clough's awareness of her husband's strength of purpose and determination to carry out his ideas, two qualities often denied him by the tradition. It is true, of course, that she talks of his "unfinished growth of mind," but it is unfair to deduce from this that she, or his friends, felt completely dissatisfied with him. As a matter of fact, an intellect like Clough's never stops growing; the situation would probably have been the same had he died ten or twenty years later. The important point is that he had thought deeply about intellectual and spiritual matters, had formed conclusions, and had put many of them into practice.

MacCarthy is inaccurate in stating that Clough was "muscle-bound" in respect to will power; rather, it was just that he refused to flex his muscles. He was determined to avoid controversy, which, he felt, never solved any problems. He refused to be a "time-server," but at the same time he did not want to start trouble merely for the sake of trouble. "The only thing to keep one quiet is the perfect readiness to be unquiet at any moment that may call for it," he once told Blanche. *(Corr.,* II, 379; *PPR,* I, 196) When these moments came, Clough was ready; but he acted rather than talked.

The same qualities that have masked his intellectual and spiritual accomplishments have also served to obscure his artistry. The self-control, sincerity, and suppressed but

pervasive emotional intensity present in the lyrics have not
yet been fully recognized. Even more regrettably, the intensity of tone, depth of insight, and sharpness of vision
present in his satire also have not been acknowledged, perhaps because of the fact that the very reasons for his success as a satirist—his subtle irony and indirect, unheroic
reformative approach—are qualities that are not rec-
ognizable from a distance. As H. F. Lowry has said,
Corydon once *had* a rival, and a very good one![2] To per-
sist in discussing the qualities of Clough's hexameters or
asking whether he is really Claude or Dipsychus is to
compound critical apathy with critical distortion, and
Clough has suffered enough from both.

In the final analysis, Clough, like Forster, has been the
victim of his own paradoxical point of view, which is to
insist that it is the writer's task to avoid absolutes and to
force upon his readers "the difficulties and complications
of the moral fact." In his insistence that life is complex,
that human nature is not only to be judged but also to be
accepted, that answers are not easily found in terms of
traditionally accepted notions and conventional attitudes,
Clough defies any established pattern and is not easily
catalogued in any one "school" or camp. In his "unremit-
ting concern with moral realism," he, like Forster, is a
maverick, even to those who pride themselves on being
liberals. Trilling writes:

> Liberalism likes to suggest its affinity with science, prag-
> matism and the method hypothesis, but in actual con-
> duct it requires "ideals" and absolutes; it prefers to
> make its alliances only when it thinks it catches the scent
> of Utopia in parties and governments, the odor of sanc-

2. Lowry, p. 22.

tity in men; and if neither is actually present, liberalism makes sure to supply it. When liberalism must act with some degree of anomaly—and much necessary action is anomalous—it insists that it is acting on perfect theory and is astonished when anomaly then appears.

The liberal mind is sure that the order of human affairs owes it a simple logic: good is good and bad is bad. It can understand, for it invented and named, the moods of optimism and pessimism, but the mood that is the response to good-and-evil it has not named and cannot understand. Before the idea of good-and-evil its imagination fails; it cannot accept this improbable paradox.

(Trilling, p. 14)

Clough, of course, could not only accept this paradox, but he insisted on writing about it. And his refusal to "play the old intellectual game of antagonistic principles" has cost him dearly so far.

The other aspect of Clough that has served to baffle the critics is his innocence, which is, of course, complementary to his recognition of good-and-evil (or, as I have termed it, his natural positivism) and his faith in the native goodness of man. It is of great interest, for instance, that Graham Greene uses as one of the epigraphs to his novel *The Quiet American* the lines from Claude to Eustace in the *Amours*:

> *I do not like being moved: for the will is excited; and action*
> *Is a most dangerous thing; I tremble for something factitious,*
> *Some malpractice of heart and illegitimate process;*
> *We are so prone to these things with our terrible notions of duty.*

(Canto II, 11. 272–275)

And in the novel itself he has his spokesman, Fowler, describe Clough as an "adult poet in the nineteenth century. There weren't so many of them." [3] Given the situation in the novel, we can see how Greene sums up perfectly the contrast between the innocence that interferes, with the constant attention to convention and its good intentions, and the adult innocence of Clough, which recognizes the harm that can come from interference based only on "terrible notions" of duty usually derived from the failure to recognize human nature for what it is and man's capacity for growth and development. "God save us always from the innocent and the good," Fowler-Greene says, and Clough would find no fault with this sentiment. To call Clough an innocent adult is perhaps not the same as calling him an adult innocent; but the quality that makes Clough attractive to Greene is one that is not found in many other nineteenth-century poets. His innocence may be the cause of his presently being misunderstood, but it will ultimately prove to be his most distinctive mark and bring him the recognition he deserves.

In one of his letters to Norton, Clough, with characteristic humor, told of a conversation between Lord Melbourne and a friend. "So-and-so is dead," the friend said to Lord Melbourne of an author. "Dear me, how glad I am! Now I can bind him up." (*PPR*, I, 239) In the same letter Clough spoke of his "figure forty" standing nearly three months behind him on the roadway, "unwept, unhonoured, and unsung; an *octavum lustrum* bound up and

3. Graham Greene, *The Quiet American,* New York, The Viking Press, 1956, p. 234. See in this connection Harry W. Rudman, "Clough and Graham Greene's *The Quiet American,*" *Victorian Newsletter,* Spring, 1961, pp. 14–15; and Lawrence Lerner, "Graham Greene," *Critical Quarterly,* V (Autumn, 1963), 217–231.

laid on the shelf." His words were prophetic, for the critical tradition has indeed bound him up and laid him on the shelf. But he is far too significant a thinker and artist to be left there. If we accept the definition of *"great satire"* as "the literary expression of a philosophical position, which blends humor and invective, as it holds up to ridicule and scorn—seeking both recognition and reform —the vices, abuses, follies, and foibles which mar man and his institutions," then Clough's satiric poetry deserves to be better known.[4] And if we acknowledge that a poet's ideas should have an important bearing on the eventual influence of his poetry, then we are safe in saying, paraphrasing F. L. Lucas's judgment of Tennyson,[5] that Clough had qualities that belong, not to this nation or to that, not to this age or to that, but to humanity at its best.

4. James Edward Tobin, "Satire: An Approach to a Definition," *The English Record,* XI (Fall, 1960), 46.

5. F. L. Lucas, *Tennyson,* London, 1957 (Writers and Their Work), p. 31.

◄ *Bibliography*

(I) PRIMARY MATERIALS

Clough, Arthur Hugh, *Poems and Prose Remains,* with a Selection from His Letters and a Memoir, ed. Blanche Smith Clough. 2 vols. London, 1869.

———, *Prose Remains, with a Selection from His Letters and a Memoir,* ed. Blanche Smith Clough. London, 1888.

———, *Selected Prose Works,* ed. Buckner B. Trawick. University of Alabama Press, 1964.

———, *The Correspondence of Arthur Hugh Clough,* ed. F. L. Mulhauser. 2 vols. Oxford, 1957.

———, *The Poems of Arthur Hugh Clough,* ed. H. F. Lowry, A. L. P. Norrington, and F. L. Mulhauser. Oxford, 1951.

Manuscript materials on microfilm and in typescript from Harvard University Library and the Honnold Library in Claremont, California.

Rugby Magazine, 2 vols. London, 1835.

(II) BIBLIOGRAPHICAL, BIOGRAPHICAL, AND CRITICAL MATERIALS

The following is an annotated selective list, chronologically arranged, of bibliographical, biographical, and critical materials on Clough.

A few items included in it have been mentioned in the first part of the bibliography, but in this section I am concerned mainly with particular portions of these items, such as the introduction. My choice of a chronological rather than an alphabetical order rests on the belief that the former will be of greater value in tracing the various directions that studies in Clough have taken and the extent of activity in any one period. Therefore, whenever the same essay has appeared in more than one place, I give the earliest source first.

KEY TO ABBREVIATIONS

AM	*Atlantic Monthly*
ASch	*American Scholar*
BNYPL	*Bulletin of the New York Public Library*
CM	*Cornhill Magazine*
CR	*Contemporary Review*
EC	*Essays in Criticism*
Ecl	*Eclectic Magazine*
ES	*English Studies*
ESat	*Every Saturday*
Fortnightly	*Fortnightly Review*
Fraser	*Fraser's Magazine*
LA	*Living Age*
LL	*Life and Letters Today*
Macmillan	*Macmillan's Magazine*
MLQ	*Modern Language Quarterly*
MP	*Modern Philology*
N&Q	*Notes & Queries*
NAR	*North American Review*
NatR	*National Review*
NBR	*North British Review*
NC	*Nineteenth Century and After*
NEc	*New Eclectic Magazine*
PMLA	*Publications of the Modern Language Association*
PQ	*Philological Quarterly*
RES	*Review of English Studies*
S	*Spectator*
SAQ	*South Atlantic Quarterly*
SR	*Sewanee Review*
TLS	*Times Literary Supplement*
VP	*Victorian Poetry*
WR	*Westminster Review*

1849

[Kingsley, Charles,] *"The Bothie of Toper-na-Fuosich,"* *Fraser,* XXXIX
  (Jan., 1849), 103–110; same in *LA,* XXI (May 5, 1849), 197–202.
  Praises the *Bothie* for its subject matter, form, and spirit.
["Review of *Ambarvalia,"*] *S,* XXII (Jan. 20, 1849), 65.
  The reviewer sees more promise in *Ambarvalia* than in the great mass
  of verses that continually come before him. The main characteristic
  of each poet is "a crude poetic power, which probably seems greater
  than it really is, from the vagueness both of subject and thought in
  which it is shrouded." This "careless obscurity" is more visible in the
  poems of Clough; Burbidge's are more complete as regards structure
  and form, but whether he has at bottom so much power as Clough
  is "a moot point."
[Whewell, William,] "Dialogues on English Hexameters," *Fraser,*
  XXXIX (March, 1849), 342–347.

1850

Rossetti, W. M., *"The Bothie of Toper-na-Fuosich,"* *The Germ,* I (Jan.,
  1850), 36–48.

1853

[Whewell, William,] "English Hexameters," *NBR,* XIX (May, 1853),
  129–150.

1861

Arnold, Matthew, *On Translating Homer.* (Section III) London, 1861.
[Hutton, R. H., and Thomas Hughes,?] "Arthur Hugh Clough.—In
  Memoriam," *S,* XXXIV (Nov. 23, 1861), 1285–1286; same in *Eclectic
  Review,* II, n.s. (Jan., 1862), 27–33; many paragraphs reprinted in
  Hutton's review of the 1869 volumes. Mainly biographical, filled with
  praise for Clough's intellectual and spiritual honesty.

1862

Arnold, Matthew, *On Translating Homer. Last Words.* London, 1862.
Bagehot, Walter, "Mr. Clough's Poems," *NatR,* XIII (Oct., 1862), 310–
  326; same in *Literary Studies* (London, 1879), II, 257–281. Bagehot,
  who knew Clough personally, spends much of his review of the 1862
  volumes discussing what he calls Clough's ambivalent spiritual and
  intellectual attitudes: "He had . . . by nature an unusual difficulty

in forming a creed as to the unseen world: he could not get the visible world out of his head." His analysis of the poetry is limited mainly to the *Amours,* which he cites as "a very remarkable description of this curious state of mind."

[Hutton, R. H.,] "Mr. Clough's Long-Vacation Pastoral," *S,* XXXV (Jan. 25, 1862), 104–105; the greater part of this review of the *Bothie* is reprinted in his review of the 1869 volumes.

[Hutton, R. H.,] "Mr. Clough's Poems," *S,* XXXV (July 12, 1862), 775–776.

In this review of the 1862 volume Hutton dwells at length on Clough's "suspense of mind," most evident in his early poetry, a quality which he condemns as "antagonistic to poetry." However, he finds the *Mari Magno* poems more harmonious and serene, showing less evidence of Clough's divided intellect; and he praises as "perhaps most perfect of all" those poems which retain *traces* of the poet's intellectual hesitancy "half-lost in a firm and certain purpose."

[Lewes, G. H.,] "Clough's Poems," *CM,* VI (Sept., 1862), 398–400.

An unfavorable review of Clough's poetry. Lewes insists that to talk of what he *might* have been, to say that he *lived* his poem instead of writing it is "mere rhetorical evasion." He cites *"Qua Cursum Ventus"* as his "nearest approach" to poetry.

Masson, David, "The Poems of Arthur Hugh Clough," *Macmillan,* VI (Aug., 1862), 318–331.

Norton, Charles Eliot, "Arthur Hugh Clough," *AM,* IX (April, 1862), 462–469; reprinted in slightly different form as "Memoir" in *The Poems of Arthur Hugh Clough.* Boston, 1862. Even more eulogistic in tone than Palgrave's "Memoir," Norton's essay describes Clough's writings as "among the most precious and original productions of the time" and Clough himself as one who "lived to conscience, not for show."

[Palgrave, Francis T.,] "Arthur Hugh Clough," *Fraser,* LXV (April, 1862), 527–536; reprinted with some changes in "Memoir" of *The Poems of Arthur Hugh Clough.* London, 1862. Same in *The Poetical Works of Arthur Hugh Clough.* London, 1906. Elegiac in spirit and eulogistic in tone. Palgrave at times shows a tendency to praise too highly both the content of the writings and the character of the subject and to pass too lightly over certain aspects of both. However, for an insight into Clough's nature and for a true understanding of the motivation behind many of his acts, the essay is valuable.

[Sellar, W. Y.,] "Clough's Poems," *NBR,* XXXVII (Nov., 1862), 323–343.

Stanley, A. P., "Arthur Hugh Clough," *London Daily News,* Jan. 8, 1862, p. 2.

1863

[Hutton, R. H.,] "Mr. Clough's Poems, New Edition," *S*, XXXVI (Oct. 10, 1863), 2604–2606; many paragraphs reprinted in his review of the 1869 volumes.

1866

Allingham, William, "Arthur Hugh Clough," *Fraser*, LXXIV (Oct., 1866), 525–535.
[Symonds, J. A.,] "Clough's Life and Poems," *CM*, XIV (Oct., 1866), 410–421; same in *LA*, XCI (Nov. 3, 1866), 259–266; same in *ESat*, II (Nov. 3, 1866), 515–520; same in *Ecl*, LXVII (Dec., 1866), 735–743.

1867

[Norton, C. E.,] "Arthur Hugh Clough," *NAR*, CV (Oct., 1867), 434–477.

1868

Symonds, John Addington, "Arthur Hugh Clough," *Fortnightly*, X (Dec., 1868), 589–617; same in *Last and First*. New York, 1919. The author, who aided Mrs. Clough with the 1869 edition of the *Poems and Prose Remains*, is one of the few contemporary writers who seem to have understood Clough's aims and ideas. Although Symonds states that he will "examine" the works, he concentrates almost solely on the *Amours*, *Dipsychus*, and *Mari Magno*. His analysis of Clough's religious position, in particular, is incisive and penetrating, and it is in this area that his understanding of the poet is most apparent.

1869

Clough, Blanche Smith, [and J. A. Symonds] "Memoir" in *Poems and Prose Remains*. 2 vols. London, 1869. Same in *Prose Remains*. London, 1888. A tender and sometimes moving memorial, containing a wealth of biographical information and supplying an interesting commentary on different facets of Clough's writings and ideas. As one might expect, the approach is mainly eulogistic; but, on the whole, the comments on Clough's thoughts and actions are surprisingly free from excessive sentiment or critical bias. The memoir still remains the starting point for any study of Clough.
Dowden, John, "Arthur Hugh Clough," *CR*, XII (Dec., 1869), 513–524; same in *LA*, CV (April 2, 1870), 56–72. In this review of the 1869 volumes, Dowden's remarks on Clough's religious position are illuminat-

ing. While not denying Clough's skeptical habit of mind (the balance of the believing and the critical), and not agreeing with Clough's final spiritual position, he insists that Clough was not a "wavering doubter," as many claim.

[Hutton, R. H.,] "Arthur Hugh Clough," *S*, XLII (Sept. 11, 1869), 1073–1075; same in *LA*, CIII (Oct. 23, 1869), 197–201; same in *Ecl*, LXXIII (Dec., 1869), 719–723; reprinted in slightly different form in *Essays Theological and Literary*, II. London, 1871. Same in *Literary Essays*. London, 1892. Hutton's review of the 1869 volumes is a satisfying, well-written one, keeping its focus on the poetry itself and exhibiting throughout a tone of objectivity. His criticism of the longer poems, especially, is sensitive and intelligent.

Robinson, Henry Crabb, *Diary, Reminiscences, and Correspondences,* selected and ed. by T. Sadler. 2 vols. London, 1869.

Sidgwick, Henry, "The Poems and Prose Remains of Arthur Hugh Clough," *WR*, XCII (Oct., 1869), 363–387; same in *Miscellaneous Essays and Addresses*. London, 1904. This review of the 1869 volumes is particularly interesting for Sidgwick's analysis of the "modern" elements in Clough's poetry.

1870

[Hutton, R. H.,] "The Modern Poetry of Doubt," *S*, XLIII (Feb. 5, 1870), 166–167; same in *NEc*, VI (April, 1870), 490–494; same in *Aspects of Religious and Scientific Thought,* selected from the *Spectator* and ed. by Elizabeth M. Roscoe (London, 1899), 380–381.

1877

Dowden, Edward, "The Transcendental Movement and Literature," *CR*, XXX (July, 1877), 309, 315–316; same in *Studies in Literature,* London, 1887.

1882

[Hutton, R. H.,] "The Unpopularity of Clough," *S*, LV (Nov. 25, 1882), 1507–1509; same in *LA*, CLV (Dec. 23, 1882), 764–767; same in *Brief Literary Criticisms,* ed. E. M. Roscoe. London, 1906. Raising the question of Clough's unpopularity, Hutton seeks the answer by contrasting the poetry of Clough and Arnold. He points out that Clough's poetry has neither the "fanciful art" nor the lucidity of Arnold's, two qualities which lead to immediate popularity. But he agrees with Lowell that in future generations Clough will rank among the highest of his time, even above Arnold, for having found a voice for his self-questioning age, a voice of great range and richness and of deep pathos.

1883

Hutton, R. H., "The Poetry of Arthur Hugh Clough," *Fortnightly*, XXXIX (June, 1883), 790–807; same in *LA*, CLVIII (July 7, 1883), 3–14.
Waddington, Samuel, *Arthur Hugh Clough*. London, 1883. Waddington's study, the first full-length volume of Clough after his death, is a disappointing work. It adds nothing substantially to the understanding of either his poetry or his life, and much of the interesting information in it is that contained in the extracts that Waddington uses from articles by authors who, as he writes in his preface, were personally acquainted with the poet.

1886

[Hutton, R. H.,] "Amiel and Clough," *S*, LIX (Jan. 9, 1886), 42–43; same in *Criticisms on Contemporary Thought and Thinkers*. 2 vols. London, 1894; same in *Brief Literary Criticisms*. London, 1906.

1889

Ward, Wilfrid, *William George Ward and the Oxford Movement*. London, 1889.

1896

Hudson, W. H., *Studies in Interpretation*. New York, 1896.

1897

Clough, Blanche Athena, *A Memoir of Anne Jemima Clough*. London, 1897.
Robertson, John M., *New Essays towards a Critical Method*. London, 1897.
Tennyson, Hallam, *Alfred, Lord Tennyson; A Memoir by His Son*. 2 vols. London, 1897.

1898

Arnold, Thomas, "Arthur Hugh Clough: A Sketch," *NC*, XLIII (Jan., 1898), 105–116. Same in *Ecl*. CXXX (March, 1898), 358–364; same in *LA*, CCXVI (Feb. 5, 1898), 382–389. The most interesting portions of this reminiscence are those in which Arnold describes Clough as he was "in the brimming fulness of his powers."

1903

Omond, T. S., *English Metrists* (London, 1903), pp. 53, 93, 95, 97, 102, 104; slightly expanded in the "recast" volume (Oxford, 1921), pp. 40, 156–157, 169n., 177–179, 284–285, 306, 308. Most of his attention is on Clough's hexameters.

1905

Brookfield, Charles and Frances, *Mrs. Brookfield and Her Circle*. 2 vols. New York, 1905.

1908

Brooke, Stopford A., *Four Victorian Poets*. New York, 1908. A generally appreciative essay supported with many excerpts from Clough's poetry by a critic who felt that the poet had too long been neglected. Brooke praises Clough's poetry for its clarity, its "ceaseless change of mood within one atmosphere," its excellent, light-flitting, kindly humour, its veracity, its intensely-felt matter.

1910

Milford, H. W., "Preface" in *Poems of Arthur Hugh Clough*. London, 1910.

1912

Lutonsky, Paula, *Arthur Hugh Clough*. (*Wiener Beitrage Zur Englischen Philologie,* Bd. XXXIX) Wien, 1912. A survey of his life and work; of interest are the points she makes regarding similarities of certain scenes in *Dipsychus* and *Faust* and the influence of the Tübingen School on his religious thought as reflected in "Easter Day," "*Epi-Strauss-ium,*" and "The Shadow."

1913

Cook, Sir Edward, *The Life of Florence Nightingale*. 2 vols. London, 1913.
Guyot, Edouard, *Essai sur la formation philosophique du poète Arthur Hugh Clough: pragmatisme et intellectualisme*. Paris, 1913.
Whibley, Charles, "Introduction" in *Poems*. London, 1913.

1918

Strachey, Lytton, *Eminent Victorians*. (London, 1918), pp. 174–175, 187 (in the chapter on Florence Nightingale) ; pp. 234–236 (in the chapter on Dr. Arnold).

1919

Osborne, James I., *Arthur Hugh Clough*. London, 1919; New York, 1920. A generally sympathetic study, but undistinguished in both its biographical and critical portions. As biography, it lacks solidity and thoroughness; as criticism it lacks depth. At best, the book may be regarded as a useful general introduction to the study of Clough's life and the general conflicts he experienced. No bibliography.

Shackford, Martha Hale, "The Clough Centenary: His *Dipsychus*," *SR*, XXVII (Oct., 1919), 401–410; reprinted with some revisions in *Studies of Certain Nineteenth-Century Poets*. Natick, Mass., 1946. Still the best study of *Dipsychus*, written by a sensitive and discriminating critic able to understand Clough's method and purpose. She recognizes the source of Clough's poetic power in his "eternal protest against spiritual ease and smugness" and analyzes *Dipsychus* from this point of view, calling it a "critique of pure worldliness."

1922

Hewlett, Maurice Henry, "Teufelsdröckh in Hexameters," *NC*, XCI (Jan., 1922), 68–75. Reprinted in *Extemporary Essays*. London, 1922. A good account of the Carlylean elements in the *Bothie*.

1923

Williams, S. T., "Clough's Prose," *Studies in Victorian Literature*. London, 1923. An essay to be read in conjunction with Beatty's (1926). Williams, unlike Beatty, finds that Clough's genius was for poetry rather than for prose; the former, particularly the lyrics, contains the record of his feelings and therefore has a certain striking inevitability. The prose, on the other hand, is stylistically undistinguished; it is laborious, self-conscious, conventional, lacks charm.

1926

Beatty, Joseph M., Jr., "Arthur Hugh Clough as Revealed in His Prose," *SAQ*, XXV (April, 1926), 168–180. The author makes a good case for the Straussian influence on Clough's religious thought and skilfully traces his advance from spiritual introspection to concern for social welfare. His conclusions concerning Clough's prose style are more open to debate.

1929

Lucas, F. L., "Thyrsis," *LL,* II (May, 1929), 344–360; same in *Eight Victorian Poets.* Cambridge, 1930; *Ten Victorian Poets,* 1940. Unsympathetic with Clough's views and unable to understand his poetic theories, Lucas is almost belligerent in his remarks upon Clough. The essay is a good example of how Clough is viewed by the critic unable to comprehend him.

Turner, Albert Morton, "A Study of Clough's *Mari Magno,*" *PMLA,* XLIV (June, 1929), 569–589. An investigation of the autobiographical elements and the influence of Chaucer and Crabbe in these last verses of Clough.

1931

MacCarthy, Desmond, "Clough," *Portraits* (London, 1931), pp. 63–67. In the dedication MacCarthy indicates that the essay was written earlier. The author attempts to "correct" the portrait of Clough, especially that painted by Strachey and Swinburne.

1932

Arnold, Matthew, *The Letters of Matthew Arnold to Arthur Hugh Clough,* ed. H. F. Lowry. New York, 1932. Lowry's introductory essay not only provides a deeper insight into the relationship between the two poets, but makes a real contribution to a better understanding and appreciation of Clough's character and thought.

Wolfe, Humbert, "Arthur Hugh Clough," *The Eighteen-Sixties,* ed. John Drinkwater. London, 1932. Dwelling on the unfulfilled promise that many saw in Clough, Wolfe supplies his own thesis as to why it remained unfulfilled. It was not religious difficulty. Rather, it was due to the struggle that absorbed and finally destroyed him, the struggle of "the innate satirical genius seeking in vain to rid itself of the swaddling-clothes of Arnoldism, and of all the honourable and clogging pieties of the period."

1934

Cunliffe, John W., *Leaders of the Victorian Revolution.* New York, 1934.
Emerson–Clough Letters, ed. H. F. Lowry and R. L. Rusk. Cleveland, 1934; superseded by Slater, Joseph, ed., Columbia University Press, 1964.

1936

Roberts, Michael, ed., "Introduction" in *The Faber Book of Modern Verse.*
London, 1936.
Scudder, Townsend, "Incredible Recoil. A Study in Aspiration," *ASch,*
V (Winter, 1936), 35–48. Reprinted in slightly different form in *The
Lonely Wayfaring Man.* London, 1936. An imaginative re-creation of
Emerson's high expectations of his English friend, aroused by his
reading of the *Bothie,* and his subsequent grief and disappointment
at Clough's later failure.

1937

Routh, H. V., *Towards the Twentieth Century.* New York, 1937. As far
as Routh is concerned, Clough "resigned himself" when he resigned
Oxford; his university career sapped his inspiration, unsettled his
thoughts, and oppressed his buoyancy and creativeness. Accordingly,
the *Bothie,* the only poem of Clough's that Routh believes worth any
consideration, takes on great significance; it becomes a symbol of
Clough's own life, partly because it is full of promise, and partly because that promise was not fulfilled.

1938

Levy, Goldie, *Arthur Hugh Clough: 1819–1861.* London, 1938. The fullest biographical study of Clough thus far, supplying details of his
movements during most of his life; the bibliography is especially note-
worthy.
MacCarthy, Desmond, "The Modern Poet," *The Sunday Times* (London),
Dec. 25, 1938, p. 6.

1939

Trilling, Lionel, *Matthew Arnold.* New York, 1939; rev. ed., 1949.

1943

Palmer, Francis W., "Was Clough a Failure?" *PQ,* XXII (Jan., 1943),
58–68. Supplies a negative answer to the question of the title, empha-
sizing that "disproportionate emphasis" has been given to Clough's
skeptical habit of mind.

1944

Palmer, Francis W., "The Bearing of Science on the Thought of Arthur
Hugh Clough," *PMLA,* LIX (March, 1944), 212–225. Palmer differs

from those who indicate that Clough was not familiar with science, and demonstrates that Clough was not unaware of the scientific movements of his day.

1945

Mulhauser, "Clough's 'Love and Reason,'" *MP,* XLII (Nov., 1945), 174–186.

1951

Badger, Kingsbury, "Arthur Hugh Clough as Dipsychus," *MLQ,* XII (March, 1951), 39–56.

Johari, G. P., "Arthur Hugh Clough at Oriel and University Hall," *PMLA,* LXVI (June, 1951), 405–425. The author supplies further information about Clough's years at Oxford and University Hall.

Norrington, A. L. P., "Preface" in *The Poems of Arthur Hugh Clough,* ed. H. F. Lowry, A. L. P. Norrington, and F. L. Mulhauser. Oxford, 1951.

"The Poetry of Clough," *TLS,* Nov. 23, 1951, p. 748. The reviewer of the 1951 edition of the *Poems* emphasizes Clough's modernity, particularly evident in *Dipsychus* and *Mari Magno.*

Woodham-Smith, Cecil, *Florence Nightingale.* New York, 1951.

1952

Dalglish, Doris N., "Arthur Hugh Clough: The Shorter Poems," *EC,* II (Jan., 1952), 38–53.

1953

Jump, J. D., "Clough's *Amours de Voyage,*" *English,* IX (Summer, 1953), 176–178. Viewing the poem as a serio-comic novel in verse, Jump finds its merits in the freedom and confidence with which the hexameter form is handled, the skillful characterization of the protagonist, and the treatment of theme in a serio-comic vein instead of the nineteenth-century tradition of "elevated" poetry.

Tillotson, Kathleen, "Rugby 1850: Arnold, Clough, Walrond, and *In Memoriam,*" *RES,* IV, n.s. (April, 1953), 122–140.

1954

Woodward, Frances, *The Doctor's Disciples.* London, 1954. A survey of Clough's life and work that is largely unfavorable in its conclusions.

Although the author had access to unpublished material, her findings
are not much different from many earlier studies on Clough.

1956

Johnson, W. Stacy, "Parallel Imagery in Arnold and Clough," *ES,*
XXXVII (Feb., 1956), 1–11.
Terhune, A. McKinley, "Arthur Hugh Clough," *The Victorian Poets:
A Guide to Research,* ed. F. E. Faverty. Cambridge, Mass., 1956.

1957

"A Searcher for the Truth," *TLS,* Dec. 6, 1957, p. 738. The reviewer of the
Correspondence, Geoffrey Tillotson, finds that the letters reveal
Clough as "one of the most searching thinkers" of his time, as a "strong
man."
Fairchild, Hoxie N., *Religious Trends in English Poetry,* IV (1830–1880).
New York, 1957.
Mulhauser, F. L. "Introduction" in *The Correspondence of Arthur Hugh
Clough,* ed. F. L. Mulhauser. 2 vols. Oxford, 1957. Rather than at-
tempting to come to any definite conclusions about Clough's life and
work in his introductory essay to the *Correspondence,* the editor
devotes much of it to pointing out various aspects that need further
study.

1958

Gollin, R. M., "Sandford's Bid for the Edinburgh Professorship and
Arthur Hugh Clough's Expectations," *N & Q,* Nov. 11, 1958, pp.
470–472.

1959

Houghton, W. E., "Arthur Hugh Clough," *Victorian Poetry and Poetics.*
Boston, 1959. A pithy introduction to Clough's life and poetry.

1960

Houghton, Walter E., "The Prose Works of Arthur Hugh Clough: A
Checklist and Calendar, with Some Unpublished Passages," *BNYPL,*
LXIV (July, 1960), 377–394. A valuable guide to many of the little
known prose works of Clough, particularly those still in manuscript
or not easily available.

1962

Armstrong, Isobel, *Arthur Hugh Clough.* London, 1962. A pamphlet in the "Writers and Their Work" series, published for the British Council.

Chorley, Katharine, *Arthur Hugh Clough: The Uncommitted Mind.* Oxford, 1962. Primarily a psychological biographical study of Clough, this work is another contribution to the long critical tradition that sees Clough a failure. Clough's chief difficulty lay "in longing with all the force of his hidden instinctive drives for complete and exclusive possession of his mother"; he had a "yearning for a return to the warmth and security of the womb."

1963

Houghton, Walter E., *The Poetry of Clough: An Essay in Revaluation.* New Haven, 1963. A valuable contribution to the understanding of Clough's poetry, especially in providing insights into its "modern" characteristics. The author's emphasis on this aspect, however, results in the lack of recognition given to Clough's moral commitment in aesthetic, intellectual, and spiritual areas and, consequently, the positive nature of his thought and art.

Ryals, Clyde De L., "An Interpretation of Clough's *Dipsychus,*" *VP*, I (August, 1963), 182–188. Disagreeing with the critics who stress *Dipsychus* as the most despairing of Clough's poems, Ryals finds it a humorous, ironic dramatization of Clough's own development. To read it as a story of failure, he concludes, is to miss the point altogether.

1964

Brooks, Roger L., "Matthew Arnold's Revision of *Tristram and Iseult:* Some Instances of Clough's Influence," *VP*, II (Winter, 1964), 57–63.

Cockshut, A. O. J., "Clough: The Real Doubter" in *The Unbelievers: English Agnostic Thought 1840–1890.* London, 1964. For Cockshut, Clough never developed "any coherent attitude" to religion, marriage, work, or life itself; and this failure is reflected in his poetry, in which he was unable to achieve "a grand, simple effect."

Trawick, Buckner B., ed., "Introduction" in *Selected Prose Works of Arthur Hugh Clough.* University of Alabama Press, 1964.

(III) SELECTED RELATED MATERIALS

Arnold, Matthew, *Culture and Anarchy,* London, 1869; ed. William S. Knickerbocker. New York, 1925.

———, *Essays in Criticism: First Series,* London, 1865; London, 1895.

———, *Essays in Criticism: Second Series,* London, 1888; London, 1894.

———, *Irish Essays and Others.* London, 1882.

Arnold, Dr. Thomas, *Christian Life; Its Course, Its Hindrances, and Its Helps.* London, 1841; London, 1849.

———, *Christian Life, Its Hopes, Its Fears, and Its Close.* London, 1842; London, 1845.

———, *Miscellaneous Works.* London, 1845.

———, *Sermons Preached in the Chapel of Rugby School.* London, 1845; New York, 1846.

Bury, J. B., *The Idea of Progress.* London, 1924.

Carlyle, Thomas, *Heroes and Hero-Worship,* in *Works,* XIV. Boston, n.d.

———, *Past and Present,* in *Works,* XIX.

———, *Sartor Resartus,* in *Works,* XIV.

———, *Signs of the Times,* in *Works,* XV.

Church, R. W., *The Oxford Movement.* London, 1891; London, 1932.

Doughty, Oswald, *The English Lyric in the Age of Reason.* London, 1922.

Drew, Elizabeth, ed., "T. S. Eliot," *Major British Writers* (enlarged ed., 2 vols., New York, 1959), II, 819–827.

Dyson, A. E., "Swift: The Metamorphosis of Irony," *Gulliver's Travels: An Annotated Text with Critical Essays,* ed. Robert A. Greenberg (New York, 1961), pp. 307–320.

Eliot, T. S., *The Use of Poetry and the Use of Criticism.* Cambridge, Mass., 1933.

Findlay, J., *Arnold of Rugby.* Cambridge, 1897.

Frankenberg, Lloyd, *Pleasure Dome: On Reading Modern Poetry.* New York, Dolphin Books, 1961.

Froude, J. A., *Thomas Carlyle: A History of His Life in London.* 2 vols. London, 1884.

Gayley, C. H., *English Poetry: Its Principles and Progress.* New York, 1929.

Harrold, C. F., *Carlyle and German Thought.* New Haven, 1932.

Hepple, Norman, *Lyrical Forms in English.* Cambridge, 1911.

Huxley, Thomas, *The Struggle for Existence in Society,* in *Evolution and Ethics.* London, 1893; New York, 1911.

Ideas and Beliefs of the Victorians. London, 1949.

Johnson, E. D. H., *The Alien Vision of Victorian Poetry.* Princeton, 1952.

Leary, Lewis, ed. *Contemporary Literary Scholarship.* New York, 1958.

Lucas, F. L., *Tennyson.* (Writers and Their Work). London, 1957.

Macaulay, Thomas Babington, *Miscellaneous Works,* ed. Lady Trevelyan. 5 vols. New York, n.d.

Mill, J. S., *Autobiography.* London, 1873.

———, *Utilitarianism,* London, 1863; New York, 1951.

Morris, William, *Hopes and Fears for Art,* in *The Collected Works of William Morris,* with introductions by his daughter, May Morris, XXII. London, 1914.

——, *Signs of Change,* in *The Collected Works,* XXIII.

Newman, John Henry, *Apologia Pro Vita Sua,* with an introduction by Wilfrid Ward. London, 1913.

Nicolson, Harold, *Tennyson.* London, 1923.

Roe, F. W., *Victorian Prose.* New York, 1947.

Ruskin, John, *Sesame and Lilies: The Mystery of Life and Its Arts,* in *Complete Works,* The Chesterfield Society ed., VI. London, n.d.

——, *The Crown of Wild Olive: Traffic,* in *Complete Works,* VII.

——, *The Stones of Venice II,* in *Complete Works,* IV.

Sanders, R. W., *Coleridge and the Broad Church Movement.* Durham, 1942.

Schmucker, Samuel M., *Life and Times of Louis Napoleon.* Philadelphia, 1882.

Shafer, Robert, "Religious Thought in England in the XVIIth and XVIIIth Centuries," *Christianity and Naturalism.* New Haven, 1926.

Sherman, Stuart P., "Poems of the Personal Life," *Matthew Arnold: How to Know Him.* Indianapolis, 1917.

Stanley, Arthur Penrhyn, *The Life and Correspondence of Thomas Arnold.* London, 1844; London, 1858.

Storr, Vernon F., *The Development of English Theology in the Nineteenth Century.* London, 1930.

Strauss, David F., *The Life of Jesus,* tr. George Eliot, with an introduction by Otto Pfleiderer. London, 1906.

Taylor, Sir Henry, *Philip Van Artevelde,* in *Works,* I. London, 1877; London, 1883.

Thompson, E. N. S., "The Octosyllabic Couplet," *Philological Quarterly,* XVIII (July, 1939), 257–268.

Thomson, David, *England in the Nineteenth Century.* Penguin Books, Harmondsworth, Middlesex, 1940.

Tobin, James Edward, "Satire: an Approach to a Definition," *English Record,* XI (Fall, 1960), 46–52.

Turner, Edward R., *Europe Since 1789.* New York, 1920.

Warren, Alba H., Jr., *English Poetic Theory, 1825–1865.* Princeton, 1950.

Williams, Raymond, *Culture and Society, 1780–1950.* New York, Anchor Books, 1960.

Williamson, Eugene L., Jr., "Matthew Arnold's 'Eternal Not Ourselves . . . ,'" *Modern Language Notes,* LXXV (April, 1960), 309–312.

——, *The Liberalism of Thomas Arnold.* University of Alabama Press, 1964.

Young, G. M., *Victorian England.* London, 1936 (rev. 1953).

❦ *Index*

A

Alexander's Feast, 105
Ambarvalia, xv
Anti-aristocratic attitude, xv, 65, 69, 74, 76–80, 150
Armellini, Carlo, 82
Armstrong, Isobel, xiv
Arnold, Dr. Thomas, xiv, 5, 23–26, 30–31, 33–35, 51, 60, 69, 74–76
Arnold, Matthew, xv, 10, 12, 20, 28, 31, 51, 72, 76, 91, 98, 102, 103, 105, 150
Arnold, Thomas (Tom), 12, 33, 76, 84

B

Badger, Kingsbury, 22
Bagehot, Walter, 12

Balance, The, xiv, 69, 70
Balliol (*see* Oxford University)
Baur, Ferdinand C., 33
Beatty, Joseph, Jr., 35, 62
Beaumont and Fletcher, 105
Bible, 20, 23, 35, 47
Bright, John, 79, 80
Browning, Robert, 28, 122, 124, 142
Burbidge, Thomas, xv, 66, 69
Buret, Eugene, 69
Burns, Robert, 105, 109
Byron, George Gordon, Lord, 96–97, 101–103, 114, 153

C

Carlyle, Thomas, xv, 5, 12, 22–23, 25–28, 30, 53, 60–62, 63, 65, 71–77, 80, 88–89, 96

Cash-nexus, 14, 63, 71, 150

Character delineation, 119, 122–130, 135, 137, 138–140, 142, 144–146, 148–149, 159–163, 165–166

Chartists, 65, 127

Child, Francis J., 137

Chorley, Lady Katharine, xiv, 5, 42, 124

Christianity, 9, 23, 29, 34–38, 43, 46, 49, 56, 59, 89–90, 101

Church of England, 20, 30, 42

Class structure, 63, 68, 73–78, 80–81

Clough, Ann Perfect, xiv, 5, 22, 23

Clough, Anne Jemima, 34, 47, 77

Clough, Arthur Hugh, Poems:
    Amours de Voyage, xv, 4, 29, 36, 37, 81, 82–83, 119, 124, 137–152, 163, 173

    "Blank Misgivings," I, 26

    Bothie of Tober-na-Vuolich, The, xv, 54, 60, 76, 77–78, 119, 125, 126–137, 138, 140, 143, 151, 163

    Dipsychus, xv, 4, 8, 15, 43, 45–46, 54, 60, 102, 119, 144, 146, 149, 152–168

    "Duty—that's to say complying," 112, 117–119, 120

    "Easter Day," 8, 29, 48–50, 59–60

    "Epi-Strauss-ium," 8, 48

    "Hope evermore and believe, O man," 54, 170

    "I dreamed a dream: I dreamt that I espied," 43–45, 112

    "I give thee joy! O worthy word!" 112, 119

    "I have seen higher holier things than these," 53–54

    "In the Great Metropolis," 112

    "Is it true, ye gods, who treat us," 112, 113–115

    "It fortifies my soul to know," 8, 29, 59, 170

    "Last Words. Napoleon and Wellington," 54

    "Latest Decalogue, The," 43, 112

    "Lawyer's First Tale, The," 55

    "Look you, my simple friend, 'tis one of those," 111–112, 119

    "Sa Majesté très Chrétienne," 112, 122–125, 145

    Mari Magno or Tales on Board, xvi, 54; *see also* 55 n. 20

    Mystery of the Fall, The, 10–11

    "O qui me—" 112, 119

    "O thou whose image in the shrine," 28

    "Qui Laborat, Orat," 26, 28, 89

    "Say not the struggle nought availeth," 170

    "Some future day when what is now is not," 170

    "To the Great Metropolis," 112, 115–117, 119

    "What we, when face to face we see," 28

    "When Israel came out of Egypt," 26, 28

    (*See also* entries for "Lyric poetry" and "Satiric poetry")

Clough, Arthur Hugh, Prose:
    Consideration of Objections against the Retrenchment Association, A, xiv–xv, 69, 74–75, 76

    "Moral Effect of Works of Satire, The," 110–111

    Notes on the Religious Tradition, xvi, 35, 46, 47, 56

    Paper on Religion, xv, 27

    (*See also* entries under individual listings and works mentioned on xiv–xvi and 94 n. 2)

Clough, Blanche Smith, xv, xvi, 36, 53, 55, 58, 170, 171

Clough, George, 23

Clough, James, xiv

Clough, Margaret, 46

Coleridge, Samuel Taylor, 69, 105, 115

"Composed upon Westminster Bridge," 115–116

Considerations on Some Recent Social Theories, xvi, 72, 80–81

Cook, Sir Edward, 58

Corrigan, Robert, 10

D

Deism, 20

Diction, 16, 103–105, 106–110, 112–117, 121, 126, 127, 152–155, 160, 167

Dissenters, 20

Dramatic monologue, 122, 142

Drew, Elizabeth, 118

Dryden, John, xv, 100–101, 102, 105

Duty, 23, 50–60, 62, 78, 87–91, 136–137, 155, 169

Dyson, Anthony E., 110

E

Education, attitude towards, 57

Education Office, xvi, 57, 58, 60

Eliot, T. S., 113, 118–119, 122, 125, 140, 149, 155, 163

Elizabethans, 104

Emerson, Ralph Waldo, 12, 61

Empedocles on Etna, 98

Epistolary method, 82, 137, 140, 141

Evangelical, 20, 33–34, 37, 40

F

Forster, E. M., 8, 11, 52, 121, 172

G

Garibaldi, Giusseppe, 82, 86

Gell, John P., 31, 57, 69

Germ, The, 127

God, 19, 23–29, 59, 90, 101, 106, 169

Goethe, 33

Goldsmith, Oliver, 105

Greene, Graham, 173, 174

H

Heroes and Hero-Worship, 95

Hexameter, 126, 137, 140–141, 144, 172

Higher criticism, 5, 20–21, 22, 25, 33–36, 46–50

Homer, 103, 126

Houghton, Walter E., 4, 114, 170

Human nature, attitude towards, 8–12, 13, 16, 23, 52–53, 59, 90–91, 101, 152, 167, 169, 170

Hutton, Richard Holt, 12

Huxley, Thomas Henry, 72

I

Imagery, 11, 16, 98, 103–105, 106, 112, 116, 123, 126, 127–136, 148–149, 155, 160, 163–166, 167

Innocence, 8, 52–53, 149, 168, 169, 173–174

Innocent hero, 126, 130, 136, 137, 143, 152, 159, 165

Irony, 110, 113, 115, 122, 137, 153, 172

J

Jowett, Benjamin, 12

K

Kant, Immanuel, 33
Keats, John, 103, 104, 105, 167

L

Labor, 63, 66–67, 69–73, 89–90
Laissez-faire, 14, 63, 66, 68–73, 79, 112
Leben Jesu, 35
Levy, Goldie, xiv
Liberal (Broad) Church, 20
Liberty, 14, 68, 79, 81, 86, 87–90
Life-Drama, A, 98, 104
Louis Philippe, 76
Lowell, James Russell, 12
Lowry, Howard F., 32, 172
Lucas, F. L., 21, 175
Lyric poetry, 16, 102, 105–109, 110, 152, 172

M

MacCarthy, Desmond, 170, 171
Macaulay, Thomas Babington, 63–65
Man's role in life, 8–12, 61, 111, 124, 125, 136–137, 138–140, 143–144, 145–149, 151–152, 155–156, 159–160, 166–167, 169–170
Maud, 124
Mazzini, Giuseppe, 82, 83, 84, 86
M'Culloch, John R., 69
Melbourne, Lord, 174
Mill, [James,] 69
Milton, John, 95, 103, 105, 109, 114, 115
Modernity, 4, 7, 15, 94, 113, 115, 117–118, 122, 140, 152–155, 160–163, 167–168
Moral aesthetic, 4, 7, 9, 13, 15–17, 95, 97, 101–103, 109–111, 169–170
Moral realism, 15, 16, 22, 52, 62, 121–122, 125, 160, 163, 165, 172
Morley, John, 66
Morris, William, 72

N

Napoleon III, Louis Napoleon, 14, 81, 85–87
Natural (opposed to artificial), 7–8, 13, 68, 96, 102, 112, 119, 125, 127–137, 143–151, 152, 159, 163–164
Newman, Francis W., xv, 12, 39
Newman, John H., 22, 23, 30, 31, 32
Niebuhr, Barthold, G., 33, 34
Nightingale, Florence, xvi, 57, 58–59, 60, 89
Norton, Charles Eliot, xv–xvi, 12, 72, 79, 80, 86, 89, 170, 174

O

"Ode: Intimations of Immortality," 120–122
"Ode to Autumn," 167
Osborne, James I., 61, 62
Oudinot, Nicolas, 82, 150
Owen, Robert, 67
Oxford Movement, 30–33
Oxford University, xiv, 5, 24–27, 29, 30–36, 48, 51, 54, 57, 61, 68, 76, 110, 132

P

Palgrave, Francis T., 76, 84

Palmer, Francis W., 21, 28, 67

Palmerston, Lord, 80

Pantheism, 20

Past and Present, 73, 74, 76, 88

Perfect, James, xiv

Poetic theory, 7, 15–17, 91–110, 167–168

Poetry of Clough, The, 4

Political attitude, 13–14, 79–87, 90, 150

Pope Pius IX, 81, 82, 86–87, 151

Positive naturalism, 7–10, 12–13, 15, 16, 36, 50–53, 60, 61, 62, 68, 90–91, 101, 119–120, 125–126, 133, 143, 163, 166–167, 168, 173

Pragmatism, 51

Protestants, 39–40

Prufrock, The Love Song of J. Alfred, 123

Puseyites (*see* Tractarians)

Q

Quiet American, The, 173

R

Religion, attitude towards, 14–15, 21–60, 62, 67–68, 89–91

Religion of Humanity, 20

Rhythmic patterns, 113, 118, 122, 126, 167; *see also* 106 n. 5

Richardson, Samuel, 141

Robertson, John M., 3, 126, 140

Roman Catholicism, 20, 37–39, 40, 44

Rossetti, William M., 127

Routh, Harold V., 21

Rugby, xiv, 5, 23, 24, 32, 34

Ruskin, John, 72, 116

Russell, Lord John, 87

S

Saffi, Aurelio, 82

Sartor Resartus, 69, 89

Satiric poetry, 6, 7, 8, 15–17, 43–46, 79, 102, 105–106, 109–168, 172, 175

Schackford, Martha Hale, 51

Schiller, Johann C., 33

Scott, Sir Walter, 96, 97, 101–102

Shairp, John C., 41–42, 55, 84

Shakespeare, 100, 114

Shelley, Percy B., 105, 114

Signs of the Times, 73

Simpkinson, John N., 31, 32

Smith, Alexander, xv, 98, 102, 103, 104, 105

Social and economic attitudes, 14, 66–78, 79, 80–81, 89–91

Sophocles, 104

Soul, The, xv, 39, 55–56

Southey, Robert, 64

Stanley, Arthur P., 12, 24, 77

Strachey, Lytton, 58

Strauss, David F., 25, 33, 35

Swift, Jonathan, 110

T

Tait, Archibald Campbell, 12

Temple, Frederick, 12

Tennyson, Alfred, Lord, 109, 175

Terhune, A. McKinley, 59

Theism, 22, 27

Thirty-nine Articles, 57

Tractarians, 5, 20, 24, 25, 30–33
Tracts for the Times, 30
Trilling, Lionel, 52, 172–173
Tristram and Iseult, 98
"True creed," 29, 46, 48, 50, 56–57
Truth, 9, 28–29, 51, 53, 100–101, 106, 169; *see also* God
Tübingen School, 33

U

Unitarianism, 20
University Hall, London, xv, 5, 57
Utilitarianism, 20, 63, 68

V

Veyriras, Paul, xiv
Victor Emanuel, 87
Virgil, 104, 126

W

Walker, Hugh, 6
Walrond, Theodore, 41, 42
Ward, William G., 31–32
Williams, Stanley T., 21
Wordsworth, William, xv, 95–99, 101–102, 109, 114, 115–117, 120–122, 154